Going Through to Get Through:

Activating your faith during life's most trying times

Rev. Kelly R. Jackson

Going Through to Get Through:

Activating your faith during life's most trying times

Copyright © 2016 by Kelly R. Jackson

ISBN: 978-0692647769

"Now the just shall live by faith; But if anyone draws back, my soul has no pleasure in him" –
Hebrews 10:38

Contents

Acknowledgements   iv

Introduction   vii

Chapter 1   Trust Him with your life: 1
Faith, purpose, and the
will of God

- *Why were we created?*   3
- *What is God's will*   6
  concerning our earthly lives?
- *The attributes of a servant*   12
- *Identifying your purpose*   18

Chapter 2   The challenge of God's   27
timing: Working your way
through the wilderness

- *How did I get here?*   29
- *What are you waiting for?*   32
- *Isolation for elevation*   35
- *The struggle to hold your*   42
  peace
- *Finding your way home*   48

Chapter 3   The ministry of marriage: 51
             What God has joined together

             • *What you want vs. what*   53
               God orders
             • *Playing your position:*   55
               Patience in the plan
             • *Everybody submits!*   59
             • *Keeping the faith while*   62
               dating
             • *Run a red light, have an*   65
               accident
             • *Remember, it's not a race*   69
             • *Trouble in paradise*   71
             • *What God has broken*   76
               apart...
             • *Marriage still matters:*   79
               Minister to someone!

Chapter 4   Going from death to life   83
             • *The lessons of mortality*   85
             • *I have a testimony*   93
             • *So how do we get up?*   100

Chapter 5   The ministry of life: Faith,   108
             finance, and applying
             God's Word

             ● *Christian crisis control:*   114
               Who says God won't put
               more on you than you can
               bear?

             ● *Bills, bills, bills (and*   121
               where your tithes fit in):
               Reconciling God and your
               finances

             ● *Knowing and*   136
               understanding Scripture

Chapter 6   The conclusion of the matter   143

             ● *The failure of faith*   145

             ● *Answering the questions*   147
               of your faith

A Final Word   153

Acknowledgments

First and foremost, I want to thank my Lord and Savior Jesus Christ for strengthening me. I want to thank Him for helping me to endure throughout this project. Surely, my faith was tested on many fronts as I was going through to get through. I thank God for being the author and using me as His ink pen. I am blessed and honored that He has chosen me as His vessel. Not a perfect vessel, but an available one. Thank you!

To my amazing wife Angela, I thank you for sacrificing your time with me for the cause of the ministry. Thank you for encouraging me whenever doubt shows up. Thank you for believing when I wasn't sure. Thank you for loving me, even when I don't come to bed on time because I've got the computer in my lap. Thank you for being an amazing mom to our son. Thank you for continuing to be a helpmeet, and not a spectator. Most of all, thank you for praying with me and praying over me. God designed you for me and I'm eternally grateful for you. Love you babe.

Thank you to my son, Daddy's Big Man, Kilen. Sometimes you make it hard for daddy to work during the day, but you also remind me of the joy that life brings. Thank you for brightening each and every day of my life. I could go on and on about how you've changed my life, and one day soon you'll be able to read and understand these words. I love you to the moon and back.

Thank you to my loving mom, Annie Loritts. Along with Angela and Kilen, I know that you're in my corner when no one else wants to be. Thank you for all that you've given me spiritually in my life. The foundation that you laid is what I'm now attempting to lay in my own family. You're the best mom God had available and I'm glad He gave you to me. I love you mom.

Thank you to my friends and family that are too numerous to name, but have supported me from the beginning.

A special thank you goes to the Zion Hill BTU Bible class! Thank you for believing in me, thank you for praying with me and for me, and thank you for pushing me to keep teaching when forces were against me. Your encouragement was more beneficial than you'll ever know. Much love to you all!

Kelly

Introduction

"Now faith is the substance of things hoped for, the evidence of things not seen." – Hebrews 11:1 (KJV)

How do we keep going when we can't see where we're going? Isn't that what we're all asking when it comes to faith? And it seems that we only ask this question when things aren't going well.

When things are alright in our lives, we're less concerned about direction. If everything is good, we don't worry. As long as we keep traveling on the same road, we expect everything to stay the same.

If there's no trouble in our marriage, the answer seems to be to keep doing what's working. Financially secure? Keep working the same job and things will continue to be fine. Don't take any chances!

In good health? Go ahead, live your life without any worries. As long as everything's okay, we don't seem to check in on our faith. We don't seem concerned with the direction we're going in.

As long as we keep living, those things are bound to change. Nobody just sails through life without having any problems, and depending on the size of the problem, what you do next has a lot to do with what you believe. At the first sign of trouble, there are many of us that just fall apart, and all of those people aren't worldly.

Many a Christian handles adversity poorly and with a sense that they have no idea where their hope is. It's alright, and even understandable, to not know what to do next. What isn't understandable for us in the Christian faith is not knowing who to turn to and not knowing that there is a solution.

As we take this journey together, I'm hoping to point you towards your hope in Christ. Faith is the linchpin of Christianity. We're asked to believe in something that we did not see, that being the death, burial, and resurrection of Jesus Christ.

We're asked to believe in someone that we can only feel, even though evidence of His existence is all around us. We're ask to trust the direction that He's taking us in at times, even when we don't know where we're going. All of these things require great faith from sometimes unsure humans.

With *Going Through to Get Through*, I hope to encourage someone that feels lost, unsure, unstable, and at times unhinged about life down here on earth. I understanding that having and exercising faith is not easy. It didn't come overnight for me, and I still have days where God has to remind me that He's in control. There are at least these four things that a Christian will encounter on this journey of faith:

- **The challenge of faith** – Having to let go of what you thought you knew, in favor of all that God knows. Trusting and believing that He not only knows what's best for you, but will provide it when the time is right. Having to take your hands off the wheel and yield total control to Him.

- **The discomfort of faith** – That uncomfortable feeling of not knowing what's next. Dealing with the fact that God said no, while waiting for the promise of something better instead.

Dealing with the ridicule of those that offer advice, while instead having to stand firm in what God said, even if it makes sense to no one but you (which is often the case).

- **The risk of faith** – What you stand to lose by standing with God. Family, friends, relationships (both romantic and otherwise), finances, jobs, and your church home are all at risk. Many times in life, we're only in certain places for a season. And then there are times when we have to step out alone, at the risk of coming back to a place and finding that the things we left behind are no longer there. You put everything at risk to follow God, while needing the faith to believe that it's all worth it.

- **The reward of faith** – After all of the faith that you've placed in God, your reward is coming. Not only your eternal reward, but God will also reward you while you're here on earth. But you must go through something to get to something. Faith is not a waste of your time and God will take care of those that

> exhibit faith, but you must be willing to endure until the end.

More than anything, I want to encourage anyone reading this book to lean on God and never give up. I hope to show that some things that we're going through aren't as bad as they seem, while other more challenging situations are still no match for God.

Whether we're talking about Christian dating, the need to pay your tithes, death, or a time of isolation and consecration, I want to encourage someone to keep the faith through it all.

Whether you read this work from cover to cover, or just start with the chapters that are speaking directly to your situation, I pray that you gain a closer relationship with God through the study of His Word and through these pages.

Please keep your Bible handy while reading it. Some Scripture is quoted, while others are just referenced. We want you to get a full understanding of what's been written.

It was my sincere pleasure to be used of God to bring you this work. I do it all for His glory, and not for any fame or fortune. I'm just happy to be in His service. In a world where so many are sitting down on God, I choose to run for Him! And even as you run, don't give up. God's got a blessing waiting for you at the end of your journey. May God bless you all as you go through to get through!

Rev. Kelly R. Jackson

Chapter 1

Trusting Him with your life: Faith, purpose, and the will of God

After confessing Christ as our Savior, our faith turns to trusting God with our lives. One would think that this is easy when we consider the fact that He is the Creator. Who better to trust than The One that breathed life into you?

However, we are created with free will and man is often arrogant enough to believe that no one can handle his life better than he can. Since The Garden of Eden, we've been trying unsuccessfully to get on God's level.

In order for us to have the right kind of faith in God, we must have a little less faith in ourselves. Sounds a little self-deprecating, doesn't it? Well, if we're going to turn our lives over to Christ that must mean that there are some things that we just can't do for ourselves.

That must mean that we aren't in control of every aspect of our lives. As Scripture tells us, we must decrease so that Christ can increase (John 3:30).

When we come to accept Jesus Christ as our Savior and become a part of the Christian faith, we're acknowledging that our way isn't the best way. We usually come to this understanding after some trial and error, and some soul searching, and not just because we're naturally inclined to trust a being that we can't see.

We come to the conclusion that we need God in our lives when we've come to some mountains that were too high to climb, or some valleys that seem too low for us to survive.

Make no mistake about it, life has a way of putting you in some positions where you can't do anything but trust in a power greater than your own. And the more you exercise your faith, the stronger it gets. The more you trust God with your life, the better you're able to handle the peaks and valleys.

You're less likely to see life as a constant struggle designed to tear you apart. When you trust God with your life, you'll begin to understand that He loves you enough to keep you through it all.

At the beginning of our faith, we're likely looking to redefine our lives. We begin to realize that we were going in the wrong direction without the presence of God. We understand that the best way to get through this life is to go through it with Jesus.

We're now ready to trust Him with our lives, which means we have to trust Him with the direction of our lives. We wanna know why we're here, what our purpose is, and how we can best serve Him going forward. After struggling in our own way, we're ready to be in God's will.

Why were we created?

Before we can even get into what God's will is concerning our lives, we must know our primary purpose in creation. God has not sent us here simply to do our own will. Again, that may seem a bit confusing considering the fact that we were created with free will. However, it is that free will that can cause us to choose greatness or choose destruction.

While God has chosen us before the foundation of the world (Ephesians 1:4-6), we must still choose Him if we wish to be saved. It may still seem odd to some that God would create us, while giving us the option of turning away from Him if we choose to.

Simply put, we were created to praise and worship God. However, this isn't just praise and worship in our Sunday morning services. In order to truly praise and worship The Lord, we must do so in every facet of our lives.

We must praise God in our day-to-day living. Our speech, our actions, and in the giving of our time, talent, and finances. In all of these areas, every Christian should be living in praise of God.

Deciding to live in constant praise of God is no simple task and shouldn't be taken lightly. Consider this: Before we go to work for a company, we should find reasons to trust them.

Is the company stable? Will I be paid a decent wage, at a scheduled time, which would enable me to survive? Will there be other benefits to working for this company (vacation time, health benefits, and other perks)?

And once I've determined whether or not the company is suitable to work for, my next step should be asking myself: Do I have the skills to perform this job? Have I been trained for this, and if not, am I willing to be? Was I created for this position at this time in my life?

If we intend to join up with God, all of these same questions should be answered. We must not only understand ourselves as God's creation, but we must understand our Creator. We must understand that He is limitless, while we have limits.

Knowing our limitations, we must come to understand what is required of us to carry out the mandate for our lives, as outlined in God's Word. Knowing that you were created to praise God means learning why He's worthy, learning where your shortcomings are *and* how to overcome them, and then committing to the task at hand.

Understand that knowing why you were created is essential in seeking to know God's will for your life. Many are under the impression that you have to be perfect in order to be in God's plan.

We're often fooled by some "super saints" into believing that once redeemed, we can sin no more, and if we do, God has no use for us. We were created in the image of God, but the flesh that we're in keeps us from achieving earthly perfection.

However, even in our imperfect state, God can and will still use us. We can still live a life of praise. Because of God's grace and mercy, we are redeemed. It is because of that redemption, the redemption that came due to no action on our part, that we should be living our lives in total praise. Our perfection has nothing to do with it, but His perfect love does.

What is God's will concerning our earthly lives?

The simple answer to this question is this: God's will is for you to prosper while living a saved life. The difficulty comes in finding out what that means.

The first thing many of us think of when we hear the word "prosperity" is financial wealth. Unfortunately, the modern church has done much to further this thought concerning prosperity. Much of our preaching and teaching has begun to focus on the material blessings of God, without focusing on the truth of prosperity in God.

When we consider the story of Job, he was a man that had wealth. However, Job's prosperity also included some intangibles. He had a strong connection with God (Job 1:8). He had good health, children, and a wife, not just possessions.

When Satan attacked Job's wealth, he didn't just take his livestock (which was the equivalent of our material wealthy today). He also took his children. He took his health. His wife was no longer supportive, as she encouraged him to curse God. His friends refused to believe that he had done nothing to offend God and began judging him. In an earthly sense, he had truly lost it all.

The point of this being that wealth isn't always found in things that can be measured. Who can place a price on the life of their child? Who can place a price on a good friend? What about your health? These are things that are invaluable.

So, while God can and will bless us with material things, it is His desire that we have wealth in all its forms. It is His desire to bless us with things that can't be quantified, and in some cases, can't be replaced. The truth about God-given prosperity is the fact that it can't truly be measured, nor can it be attained by man without God's intervention.

As we move through our earthly lives, God wants us to succeed, but not without some challenges along the way. We're all more appreciative of the things we have to earn in life through hard work, sacrifice, and/or struggle, and God knows this.

Some of the things we struggle with as Christians are tests and trials. We want the prosperity of life, but we often want God to bless us just for being alive. We don't always want to put effort behind our prayers.

But even as God wants us all to prosper, if there's no effort to go with your faith, doesn't God just become a genie, and not what Hebrews 11:6 says He is, which is "a rewarder of them that diligently seek Him"?

To be diligent is to be attentive and consistent, and to pursue with great perseverance. In order to diligently seek God, you must seek all things about Him. It is a daily task.

We mustn't pencil God into our day, but rather we should put Him on our schedule with permanent marker. He can't be an option. He must be THE priority. Once we seek Him in this manner, we begin living a saved life. Once we do that, we understand just how blessed and how prosperous we really are.

***

However, in our effort to pursue God and His will for our lives, we'll undoubtedly suffer some loss along the way. The question arises: How can a loving and giving God that wants us to prosper allow the suffering that comes with financial struggles, relationship struggles, family struggles, or the loss of loved ones? If it is in fact His will for me to prosper, why doesn't He keep me from these types of setbacks?

In the midst of our Christianity, we often lose track of our humanity. We're saved and we understand that this world is not our final destination, but we forget that those facts don't make us immune to the struggles and difficulties of life. We forget that being saved doesn't cause us to be trouble free.

If everyone else has problems, we will too for as long as we're alive on earth. However, the prosperity in your struggle is in the faith that you develop in the God that can and will deliver you from setbacks, and the strength that you gain from having to endure.

One of the biggest misconceptions in the Christian community is that those that are prosperous have an abundance of "things". While it's true that having an overflow is a level of prosperity, so is having enough to meet your needs. We often forget two critical points:

1. When you're blessed in the overflow, those blessings are to spill over (overflow) to someone less fortunate. Remember the parable of the prosperous man that wanted to build bigger barns, rather than help someone with his prosperity (Luke 12:16-21)? All of his possessions were for naught when God required his soul.

2. Those of us that are simply having our needs met may not feel prosperous, but to someone that's homeless or living in a shelter, we look like kings and queens. Prosperity is often like beauty, it's in the eye of the beholder. Our needs being met is squarely in the will of God and is definitely a level of prosperity.

As God prospers us, it's in His will for us be strong in Him and to be able to handle life's most difficult storms with great perseverance. You can't become strong in The Lord if you never have to call on Him in times of trouble. Those that are godly prosperous are strong.

In the midst of trouble, they know it won't last forever because God has brought them through before. In the midst of triumphs, they know that it was nothing but God's grace and mercy that was behind their achievements.

Therefore, God's will is for you to thrive in all situations, through your dependence on Him. While it won't always be easy, we will always be victorious if we continue to trust God.

"35 Therefore do not cast away your confidence, which has great reward.

36 For you have need of endurance, so that after you have done the will of God, you may receive the promise." – Hebrews 10:35-36 (NKJV)

The attributes of a servant

What we've described so far in this chapter as it pertains to why we're created and being in God's will, is a servant. So if you plan on being in His will, you must be willing to *do* His will.

Understand that a servant isn't one that brings self-importance into the equation. Their only desire is to please their master. They don't have agendas. Their only agenda is their master's agenda. Even if what their master asks them to do goes against what they want to do or would normally do, they will acquiesce to their master's will.

This is to our detriment when sin is our master. The Apostle Paul talks about this battle between the flesh and the spiritual mind in Romans 7:14-25. When you're a slave to your flesh, sin is in fact your master and you will do as your master tells you. But the change comes with a made up mind to do God's will and live according to His Word.

As the Word of God states in Matthew 6:24 and in Luke 16:13, you can't serve two masters without coming to hate one. There must be a change in our thinking if there is to be a change in our living.

In order for man to be free from an oppressive master, he must first be free in his mind. As the Apostle Paul closes out Romans Chapter 7, he states in Verses 24 and 25:

"24 O wretched man that I am! Who will deliver me from this body of death?

25 I thank God – through Jesus Christ our Lord! So then, with the mind I myself serve the law of God, but with the flesh the law of sin." (NKJV)

When we become servants of God, we are becoming servants of a Master that knows and wants what's best for us, even when we don't quite understand the direction. But as we often refer to ourselves in the Christian community as servants of God, do we really understand what a servant is?

In our flesh, as we're living in a secular world, we're often encouraged to achieve and succeed. We often want to be at the head of everything. But how can we really serve if we're always looking to be in a position of authority?

In order to truly be of good service to God, we must have a spirit of humility. So how can we ever claim humility if we don't have the intestinal fortitude to sacrifice our wants for the needs of others? How will we ever swallow our pride for the greater good if we're only willing to see what's good for us?

To be in the business of being a servant we must be willing to trust The Master with what we're willing to sacrifice. To be a servant of God, you must be firmly invested in the business of faith.

As we submit to serving God, we submit to serving others. The ultimate sacrifice comes in putting our needs second, our ideas on the back burner for someone else's idea that happens to be better, and to give from our place of comfort to someone that's in a place of desperation.

We can't have an attitude that suggests that we will only serve God, but we can't help our fellow man in their time of need. We must know that in order to serve God, we must serve one another.

The Apostle Paul often referred to himself as a prisoner of The Lord. He was under God's orders. That same mentality can be applied to those of us that suggest that we're servants of God.

A servant, or even a slave, doesn't have a will of their own. Their desire is to do the will of their master. We as Christians should have a desire to do the will of our Master, and that will include doing for others, whether they be friend or foe.

***

Our model for service to God is none other than Jesus Christ. It is in the Garden of Gethsemane that Jesus, while faced with certain death, submitted to the will of God above His desire to "let this cup pass from me" (Matthew 26:39).

Even facing death, He was willing to do as The Father willed. Even as He was taken into custody, beaten, bruised, spit upon, disgraced, and eventually nailed to the cross and crucified, He died for those that were committing these atrocities against Him. Why? Because He was serving God and doing His will, and not serving man and his will, nor the desires of His own flesh.

How does this apply to us? We're often called upon to be in service to The Lord by doing for people that are unappreciative. We're often called upon to do things for people that have wished us ill and slandered our names. People that have done all that they could to try and destroy us.

One of the most difficult things a Christian will ever have to do is to serve someone that has done nothing but try to bring them down. Someone that probably wouldn't serve them if the roles were reversed. But if Jesus can die for those mocking Him at the foot of the cross, what excuse do we have for not serving those that seem as if they don't deserve it?

When we're in service to God, we must always keep our perspective. As we run this race, we must remember Hebrews 12:2-3:

"2 Looking unto Jesus the author and finisher of our faith; who for the joy that was set before Him endured the cross, despising the shame, and is set down at the right hand of the throne of God.

3 For consider Him that endured such contradiction of sinners against Himself, lest ye be wearied and faint in your minds."
(KJV)

We must remember that in order to do God's will, and in order to be God's servant, we must serve God's people. In serving His people, we are serving Him. As long as we remember that, we can continue to do as God would have us to do. Remember that even when man isn't worthy of the effort, the God that we serve always is.

Identifying your purpose

I host a weekly radio broadcast in Detroit called "Your Life with Purpose". I begin each broadcast reading what I call the declaration for the broadcast, which is found in Romans 8:28:

"28 *And we know that all things work together for good to those who love God, to those who are the called according to His purpose." (NKJV)*

Once I'm done reading the Scripture, I always stress that we are called according to God's purpose, and not our own.

As we have discussed the will of God in this chapter, when we're searching for our purpose in this earthly life, it's natural for us to become a bit selfish. We want to know our purpose, but we want to know how that purpose will benefit us. Not always how we can serve man, but rather how we can prosper ourselves.

Romans 8:28 is one of the most popular verses in the Bible, but why? When we think of all things working together for good, are we fully understanding what that means?

As popular as this verse is, it's also often misquoted. People will often take the words "all things work together for good" and change them to "all things work together for *my* good". This is why the study of Scripture is so important. One word can change the entire context in the text. (More on this text later)

Here it is again: The purpose of man is to do God's will. It is to serve God in all things. When we find ourselves searching in life for a purpose, it's important that we seek God before seeking our own goals, dreams, and desires.

Many people that feel lost concerning their purpose are often that way because there's too much of *them* in the purpose. We haven't always fully submitted to what it is that God wants for our lives.

What that means is, if I really want to achieve my purpose in life, I'll do whatever God wants, wherever I am, and in whatever season I'm in. To use myself as an example, as a writer, I'm good with my words. I've also written a book of poetry, which means I have an extensive imagination. However, some of my work is politically charged, filled with emotion, and calls for a great deal of self-examination.

For profit, I could've easily taken the road of romance writer and poet, and cornered the market on selling books that women would've bought in great numbers. But as Scripture tells us, what does it profit a man to gain the whole world and lose his soul (Matthew 16:26, Mark 8:36)?

I had to accept the fact that God wasn't calling me to pull on the heart strings of the world as much as He was calling me to write about salvation. He was calling me to write about His Word. He was calling me draw people to Him.

My desire had to surrender to His purpose for my life. Do I desire to be a bestselling author? Absolutely. But my greatest desire is to do things as He has ordered. By doing that, God has given me a joy that could never be found in the finance and fame of succeeding in something that He hasn't ordained.

Where we struggle in purpose is in accepting the truth that God will grant us the desires of our heart while we're doing something that we may not have chosen to do on our own, but He has ordered. The Bible tells us to do all things to His glory (1 Corinthians 10:31), so when we're seeking our purpose, we should ask ourselves three questions:

1. **Is what I'm doing pleasing to God?** – Don't concern yourself with whether or not you're happy before you make sure that God is happy. Remember, a servant doesn't have a will of their own. Your job as a servant is to please your Master. Find your happiness in pleasing God. If it's all about what you want, you're no longer His servant. You are your own servant.

2. **Is God being glorified in my deeds and my efforts?** – Are you doing what you're doing so that God might be glorified, or are you looking for your own glory? In searching for our purpose, we must remember that it is God that glorifies us (Romans 8:30), so we needn't seek such things from man. Man's glory is fleeting and often changes based on their need. Because God doesn't have need of anything from us, what He gives is genuine.

Also, God is looking at the attitude in our effort. When Scripture tells us that God loves a cheerful giver (2 Corinthians 9:6-7), that isn't in finance only. If you're serving God according to His purposes, God expects you to do so with joy in your hearts. We shouldn't do anything that God has called us to do grudgingly just because we're in a place that we didn't envision. You may not be where you want to be, but praise God that He has placed you where He would have you to be.

3. **Is what I'm doing of service to my fellow man?** – If your purpose is aligned with God's purpose for your life, whatever He has called you to do will no doubt help your fellow man. While what God has for you to do may not help all men, it will help whom God has determined for you to help.

Again, if it's all according to God's purposes, there is no selfish end to it. God was so giving that He in fact gave us His son as the propitiation for our sins (1 John 4:10). If God can give so great a gift as Jesus, He expects us to use our gifts, talents, and abilities to benefit others, and not just ourselves.

So our purposes aren't wrapped up in what we accomplish for ourselves, but rather what we accomplish for the Kingdom of God. This is the essence of everything working for good, and not necessarily just our particular good. Our good should be tied in to what's good for mankind.

So if you've been gifted with the ability to generate millions of dollars in income, God has a divine purpose for that ability that He's given you. It isn't for mansion building, but rather Kingdom building.

If God hasn't given you that gift, but He instead gave you the ability to serve your community, it isn't so that one day they can erect a building in your honor, but rather so that honor can be attached to God's name for the work you've done through Him to help others.

No gift is greater than the other, but they're all given from God so that He may be glorified in our living. If we really want to serve God's purposes, and thus find our own, we must look to others.

As we talked about prosperity and God's will for man earlier in this chapter, one would have to wonder, are we outside of God's will when we have so many that are homeless and hungry here in America? The answer, as far as I'm concerned, is yes.

No one that claims Christianity should feel comfortable drowning in wealth when so many are drowning in poverty. Not that we shouldn't achieve wealth when we're able to, but we should always do so with a heart and mind to spread that wealth to those less fortunate.

We are God's hands, so our purpose is tied to those that are in need of our assistance. Who has a need that we can fill? Who can benefit from what we know, what we can teach, what we can do, and what we can give?

***

Many of us are great at things that we're trying not to do because it clashes with *our* plan for our lives. So many of us can't accept the fact that God didn't call all of us to be financially rich.

Many of us struggle with the fact that we're called to work on God's ground floor and not in man's penthouse. But those that are really about what God would have them to do aren't as wrapped up in where He has them positioned, as much as they are in the fact that He chose to place them where He wanted to. They're just happy to be on the team.

They're just trusting and believing that God has them right where He wants them to be so they can make the impact that He would have them to make.

God's will for our lives, our purpose while we're here on earth, and the joys of being His servant and His alone will all be revealed as we grow in our understanding. The growth comes when we cease trying to develop our plan and begin trying to understand His.

What God wants for us is spelled out in His Word. While we're trying to figure it out, He's already worked it out. He's already planned it out. He's already ordered our steps. Even when it feels as if we're traveling in darkness, He's the light at the end of the tunnel.

As we forge ahead on this Christian journey, we must remember that even in our struggle to stay the course, even in our struggle to praise God in times of trouble, even when we as servants don't understand the direction that The Master is sending us in, we must trust His plan for our lives and the purpose for which we are created.

Know that when you love someone, their joy becomes your joy. So if we love God, we should desire to please Him in our living. And when we give God joy, He's sure to return it.

Chapter 2

The challenge of God's timing: Working your way through the wilderness

"Wait on The Lord: be of good courage, and He shall strengthen thine heart: wait, I say, on The Lord." – Psalms 27:14

We all feel as though waiting on God is the hardest part of life, but it's also a necessary part of life. Often, there's a gap between what we've asked for and what we're ready for.

Sometimes we're godly ambitious, but fleshly committed. Meaning we've asked God for a level of blessings, freedom and responsibility that we're just not ready to handle. For this reason, God works on His time and not ours.

Then again, there are those times when God gave us opportunity, we squandered it, and now we're waiting for the blessing to come back around.

It's true, sometimes God will yield to the will of man just to make a point. Sometimes we get exactly what we asked for, and when we screw it up, we wonder if we'll ever get the chance again. Thank God for His grace and mercy. He's not a God of a second chance, because if that were the case, we'd be done. We need to give Him praise because He's the God of *another* chance.

The Verse heading this chapter tells us to wait on The Lord. And, to quote my dear mother, "By the end of the Verse, it tells us to wait yet again". I imagine that this is repeated because God knows we're impatient.

God knows that once He begins a movement in our lives, we don't ever expect Him to pause. We all believe that salvation puts us on the fast track. However, there are times when God will halt things. He's not pacing Himself. He's pacing us.

As God is pulling us out into the wilderness so that we can be prepared for what it is we feel we're ready for, we're going to look around at some point and notice that our surroundings have changed.

Some people are missing, our support appears to be lacking, and though we feel as if we're heading into the right direction because God is leading, not only do we feel lost, but folks are beginning to question whether or not we know what we're doing. Make no mistake, being in the wilderness has many questions. But God has all the answers.

How did I get here?

The strangest thing about being in the wilderness has to be the fact that nobody ever plans to be there. When we start out on our journey, the plan is to reach our destination as quickly as possible, and with very few distractions and detours.

Think about when we go on road trips. We map out the quickest route and we even leave at certain times so that we can avoid traffic. However, there is always the chance of unforeseen eventualities.

When we find ourselves in our own personal wilderness, a place where we didn't plan to be, those unforeseen eventualities are what frustrate us so much. Those things that have us scratching our heads and trying to figure out which way to go next are what threaten our sanity.

This is particularly true when we feel as if we were following God's direction. To end up somewhere feeling lost and alone is a true test of our faith because sometimes God has just brought us through a Red Sea-type situation, so we not only know that He's there, but we know that He cares for us. And if that's the God we're following, how do we end up lost?

Let's deal with the idea of being lost for a moment. As Christians, we should stop referring to a wilderness experience as being lost. From a Christian perspective, the only time a person is lost is when they're unsaved.

A Christian can never be lost as long as God knows where they are and He has His hands on them. Just because man is unaware of where you are, that doesn't mean that God is unaware. When we consider the Children of Israel, after crossing the Red Sea, they were lost as far as their own understanding, but they were never out of God's sight.

Sometimes we find ourselves thinking just as those Israelites did, that God has led us to a place just so that we can die. We felt that tugging in our spirit that told us to go into the ministry, or start our own business, or chase a dream that no one understands but us, or even go into the inner city to work with underprivileged children when our degrees could've gotten us a nice, cushy job in the suburbs.

We felt all of those things and we believed that it was God sending us in a certain direction. So when we get stuck, when we find ourselves alone, when we feel as if we're lost without a clue of which way to go, we wanna know, "How did I get here?"

You can begin to answer that question by always understanding that God's direction *and* His directive are divine. If God led you to a place, He's leading you to a purpose. Even if you look around and the place seems desolate and alone, you'll find that God will still sustain you day after day.

If you wanna know how you got to a place of isolation for God's purposes, it's because God sent you there. Now that you're there, the soul searching can begin.

What are you waiting for?

When we're trying to answer the question of why God brought us to a particular place, we must first examine ourselves. It's so easy to begin questioning God and asking Him why we're in a certain place or what we're supposed to do now, but the first questions belong to us.

God may have in fact pointed us in a certain direction, but did we take the route that He told us to take? Did we go through the people that He told us to go through, or did our pride or our feelings about that individual cause us to use someone that God hadn't authorized?

Did we commit to the vision that He gave us, or did we alter it? Most importantly, when we received that vision from a holy God, did we alter our living to coincide with living out the promise given to us by a holy God?

When you examine those questions for your own life before questioning, or even blaming God for why you have to wait in the wilderness, you may in fact find that it was never God's plan for you to wait. Know that God's blessings on your life aren't yours no matter how you're living.

When you ask God for a blessed destiny and He agrees to give it to you, you can't continue on living however you want. God expects us to live up to the call *and* the blessings.

Also, you may find that it was God's plan for you to go through some trials so that you might know that He delivered you, and so that you can appreciate your blessings when you reach them. All that you're doing may have been designed for you to exercise your faith and for you to grow in that faith.

Consider again the Children of Israel. God could've made a way for Moses and the Israelites to escape captivity without ever having to confront Pharaoh. But by having to deal with Pharaoh head on, all were able to see that God's power can deliver us without us ever having to cower in the face of those that wish to oppress us.

When they crossed the Red Sea, it wasn't God's desire for them to spend 40 years in the wilderness wandering. The journey from the wilderness to the Promised Land would've normally taken only a few weeks. It was their disobedience and lack of faith that kept them from reaching their destination sooner.

God's promises to us are real, but we sometimes need to evaluate our commitment to God. There are times when we're more committed to the promise than we are to the God of the promise. We want to go from point A to B, but God may want to add a few more letters to the equation.

God sometimes wants to refocus us on why it is we started out. So often we're in this wilderness state looking to God and asking "What's the holdup?" In the meantime, God is looking down at us and asking the same question.

There are times when God will slow progress because we're moving in the wrong direction, or we're moving in the right direction, but we're skipping steps. There are also times when God will stop progress because we've stopped progressing. As we're waiting patiently in the wilderness, we must also remember to wait FAITHfully!

We must remember to never give up on God just because traffic has momentarily stopped. There's a plan, a path, and a purpose. But if you're not moving, don't always assume that God has stopped working on your behalf. Sometimes, we've stopped working on His behalf. Sometimes, all you're waiting on is you.

Isolation for elevation

Whether you're in favor of the wilderness or not, you must understand that it's all a part of God's plan. It may not feel like it, it may not look like it, and it may be counter to what you thought God promised you, but know that it was always a part of God's plan for us to be isolated before we're elevated. This time of consecration is necessary if we're to be what God would have us to be at the next level.

As God looks to shape and mold us into what He wants us to be, we must also understand that there is some reshaping that must go on as well.

So those of us that are passionate, but only passionate about sinful things, God wants to redirect our passion, not take it away from us. For those of us that are intellectuals, but only for worldly causes, God needs our intelligence, but He needs it focused on Him.

Those of us that are talented and gifted, but have used those talents and gifts for the world, God doesn't want us to lay our talents down, He just wants us to use them for His glory.

When we come to God from the world or from a place where we weren't in His service, we must understand that we have some things on us that must be removed. We have some habits, some ways, some addictions, and some behaviors that are not of God. Before we can truly be used for God's purposes, these things have to be stripped away.

The easiest way to stay in a rut is to stay in the place that got you stuck. So when God calls us up and out for greater service, He's going to call us out of the rut of former friendships, former family relationships, former jobs, former romantic relationships, and even former church relationships.

When He isolates us in the wilderness, He's taking the time to strip us of all of our old allegiances in order to form some new alliances. When God is taking you to something new, you can't be beholden to what's old. Sometimes God has to break us apart in order to remake us into what He wants us to be.

When those Children of Israel had been in captivity all of those years, as much as they loved God, they had still taken on some characteristics of their oppressor Egypt. It's been said that it took one night to get them out of Egypt, but it took 40 years to get Egypt out of them.

When we've been living in the world, following the edicts of the prince of darkness, we have some stuff on us. God can't just elevate you to a Promised Land or a holy position just as you are. He's got to have some alone time with you so that He can shape you into a vessel that He can fill, so that you may pour out into others.

Whether you're in the world or in God, you'll never be able to succeed by carrying everyone and everything that you used to. Success never comes without sacrifice. As you're going through the wilderness, God is going to change some things for your benefit and for His use:

Friends – When God starts pulling you in a different direction, you quickly come to understand the difference between friends, acquaintances, and enemies.

People that claimed that they would support you no matter what easily become people that will only support you if you're going in the same direction they are. Some people just need a partner in crime, but the moment you try and go legit, you see that the love wasn't there like you thought.

You'll also find out, particularly in the church, that many love you when you're next to them in the pews, or even sitting there as they minister. However, the moment God calls you up front, they make you aware that they don't approve of what God has done in your life.

This is why God wants to isolate you. So that you come to understand where your help is really coming from, and it's never from the place where you thought it was. In time, you find out that God will send new friends and new supporters, often from unexpected places.

Family – I've often stated that we've allowed the enemy to change and distort the meaning of the word "family". The word used to invoke feelings of warmth, togetherness, unity, and support. Never just bloodline.

However, as time has gone forward, we've all come to realize that some of the worst people in the world are actually some of our blood relatives, and they're not just people in someone else's family. And we've said, "Well, that's just family." But God says "Not so."

Understand that as God isolates you for elevation, you're going to find out just how many of your blood relatives are not on board with your call. It's surprising to those that haven't read what Jesus said about it or even what happened to Him personally (Matthew 13:57-58, Mark 6:3-6, John 7:3-5), but even when you know it's coming, it still hurts.

However, God wants us to know that in the midst of it all, family is about bond, not blood. Therefore, even as you lose people that you feel should've supported you, God will send you the right people to bond with in the truest spirit of brotherhood and sisterhood.

Associations – Some of the people that we even casually associate with can be a hindrance to what God has for us to do. Sometimes we feel because we're not in deep with some people that they can't harm the work we're doing.

However, anything or anyone that distracts us from the purpose that God has for our lives is a threat to our success. God wants all of the distractions, especially ungodly ones, taken away. Even those that appear minor.

Location – How about this? Sometimes we only wanna do what God told us to do where we wanna do it. However, there are times where God will call us out of where we're comfortable, to do a work for people that need our gifts, even though we know nothing about them.

We often wanna stay close to home so that what we're excited about in God can benefit the people we're close to and grew with. But understand that just as we referenced Jesus not being received by His family, some people that you're close to will have to realize God's vision for your life from a distance.

***

Such changes are often rapid in our lives, and come upon us suddenly. God isn't trying to damage you, nor is He trying to ruin lifelong bonds that you have formed. When God isolates us, He simply wants us to be made over into what He would have us to be.

Most times, we resist God's every effort unless He takes us out of certain situations, out of certain locations, and definitely away from certain people. Again, if we intend to live out God's promises, we must do so God's way. In order to teach us that way, God sometimes needs our undivided attention so that what He's teaching can be learned and applied.

Once God is done, He may return you to the people that He removed you from. Not so that you can revert and not so that you can gloat, but so that they can see the new creature that you are.

It is during these moments that you find out who understands God's work and who recognizes His hand over your life. Once God has turned a life around for the purposes of elevation and Kingdom work, you find out who really accepts the fact that God uses whom He wants, and not whom we choose.

Not all will accept you. Not all will applaud you. As you were isolated, these were some of the very people that called you "funny acting". They'll tell anyone that will listen that they don't trust your transformation.

In fact, those most likely to resist the call on your life are those in your family and those in your church. They knew you when you were a slave. They knew who you were before God changed you.

Just as it is with becoming saved, they've given you a life sentence in the prison that was "who you used to be". But just as God did with those Israelites, He broke the bonds of your slavery, and whether the naysayers believe it or not, there's a greater work for you to do in Christ.

The struggle to hold your peace

As we go forward to do what God has called us to do, we'll find that people will put up resistance for all kinds of reasons. Remember, not everyone in your life is a cheerleader, urging you on to victory. While it would be nice to see people live and let live as long as what another is doing isn't harming them, the truth is folks don't always operate that way.

The sad part in this is eventually, those people begin to attack you. Sometimes because of jealousy, sometimes because of resentment, sometimes because they don't approve, and most times because they're under the influence of the enemy. These attacks are just costs associated with God's elevation.

Something I shared on my weekly radio broadcast, "Your Life with Purpose", is people will take shots at you once you're elevated, because once you're elevated, you're easier to see. This is often what shocks us because we have no idea about how people feel about us being in leadership until God actually places us in that position.

When God separates you for a specific assignment, you're no longer just blending in with the crowd. To take a shot at you in crowd may mean hitting the wrong target. Things that are elevated are obviously more visible and are often easier to hit, even if they're hard to destroy. When we're separated and elevated, we're immediately candidates for target practice. But if you're in Christ, you're bulletproof.

***

One of the challenges we will face during times like these is the challenge to hold our peace. When you're under attack, it's instinctive to want to fight back. Nobody wants to be beat up on, especially by fellow "Christians", for simply walking in the call that God has placed on their lives.

When shots are fired, it's natural to want to shoot back. But if we're to be successful, we have to lean on God's Word, and He hasn't called us to do His work without a plan to protect us from evil doers (Psalms 37:1-2).

As a personal testimony, when I was called into the ministry, there were some in my home church that were loudly against it. You would've thought that raising a preacher would've made them proud, but not so. For the life of me, I couldn't understand why people in a church wouldn't want a man to preach, unless his doctrine was flawed or his living was overtly sinful.

Even if they thought I didn't know enough, it would seem as if they would've prayed for me as I learned (I enrolled in school a year before announcing my call). I wasn't surprised by *who* spoke so loudly against me, but it was still disappointing considering the fact that we're all supposed to be about The Kingdom, and not our opinions.

There were even times when I was preached against from the pulpit by fellow ministers, and yet, the real challenge I faced wasn't what was being said. The real challenge I faced was in how I would respond.

The man in me wanted to address everything that was said about me, which would've been catastrophic and not what God wanted. However, the God in me kept reminding me that this is not my battle. God called me, so He would defend me.

> *"Ye shall not fear them: for The Lord your God He shall fight for you." – Deuteronomy 3:22 (KJV)*

When you're being beaten on, particularly in the church, you feel isolated. You feel like you're on an island and no one understands what you're going through, and quite honestly, many don't.

People are mocking you for the pleasure of others, and it seems as if the devil is having a good laugh at your expense. You wanna walk away, but God keeps telling you to stay put. Even though there's plenty of people around, you feel as if you're alone in the wilderness.

When you're in a position like this and you're struggling to hold your tongue, you must remember that God's Word still remains true. In the midst of an attack on you, remember that every action doesn't necessarily require a reaction.

You can't control what's done to you, but you can control how you respond. I'm drawn to one of my favorite passages of Scripture, which is Galatians 6:7-9:

> **"7 *Be not deceived; God is not mocked: for whatsoever a man soweth, that shall he also reap.***

8 *For he that soweth to his flesh shall of the flesh reap corruption; but he that soweth to the Spirit shall of the Spirit reap life everlasting.*

9 *And let us not be weary in well doing: for in due season we shall reap, if we faint not."* *(KJV)*

The key to holding your peace is remembering that God has to deal with you according to your actions. No matter what anybody does to you, God will deal with their actions *and* your reaction to it.

They will reap what they've sown as it relates to how they've treated you, but so will you if you respond in the same manner. We must remember to sow good so that we might reap that which is good. We must continue to do well and trust God with the outcome.

Those that are attacking you are doing so because they're still slaves to the flesh, which is corruption. However, there is a blessing in not retaliating.

God has told us how to handle those that are against us in Romans 12:9-21. He's told us to overcome evil with good. He has said that vengeance is His and His alone. We're not in the get even business, we're in the get righteous business. Do the best you can to get along with those that are seeking to destroy you, and the best way to do that is to keep silent and let God speak for you.

Finding your way home

It's common for Christians to feel lost on their journey. This is something that we aren't taught often enough in the church. We must tell our people that Christianity isn't some bed of roses, and often we're under attack from within.

The people of the church do more damage to one another than anyone on the outside ever does. For that reason, the only times we feel lost and isolated aren't because God is separating us. That feeling also comes because of how we treat one another.

Whether you're isolated by God or isolated by man, you can find your way back home again. In either situation, God doesn't intend for us to be isolated forever. As stated earlier, we're only "lost" based on our own perception of the situation. At all times, God has His eyes and His hands on us. The wilderness is a place of great growth as long as we allow God to cultivate the area. It can be a place of great reshaping as long as we allow God to have His way.

Home isn't necessarily the place we started from or even the place we planned to be when we started our journey. Home is wherever God intended for us to be.

As we search for our own personal Promised Land, we must remember that finding our destination and seizing that destination are two different things. Once the Children of Israel got to the Promised Land, they had to possess it. Even though God promised it to them, it wasn't just handed over to them. So even going into battle, those that had faith and trust in God knew they would be victorious.

As you go forward from whatever your wilderness experience may be, know that whatever God has promised you will be. Even when you feel lost, stuck, attacked, abused, or just plain unappreciated, know that God is making a way. He hasn't brought you here to die. He's brought you here to turn you into what He purposed for your life from day one.

God has taken this alone time with you so that He can rid you of the chains of slavery that once held you back. A new destination requires a new creature in Christ.

Elevation requires evolution. And even when we've already been in service to God, sometimes He takes us to new heights. Heights where our old skill set is no longer useful, and we must shed that to be effective at the next level.

Even as people are fading into the background of your life, even as God is moving you from one location to another, even as He's changing you from what you used to be to what you need to be for His service, trust the plan, trust the path, and trust the process.

<u>Chapter 3</u>

The ministry of marriage: What God has joined together

Most people in the Christian faith are aware of what The Bible defines as God's plan for marriage. We know that He created one woman for one man. While society has gone in a different direction, we know what God's Word says. We also know that The Bible says that what God has joined together, no man should put asunder (into separate parts) (Genesis 2:24, Matthew 19:4-6).

However, knowing what God says doesn't necessarily mean that we're all in agreement with how perfect His plan is. Over the years, we've all decided that we know what's best for our own love lives, even in the face of what Scripture says. But when you look at the number of failed or failing marriages in the world, it serves as proof that we're getting it wrong.

Even in the church, we're failing to put emphasis on what it is that God says about marriage. For fear of being unpopular, we've remained silent as the idea of marriage is ignored. People are leading ministries in the church while living beneath what God has ordered, and we're afraid to speak on it (but that's another book for another time).

God's plan for marriage, just like His infallible Word, isn't in need of any updates, tweaks, or modifications. When just need to teach it. We just need to live it.

I firmly believe that the people of God still desire to be married. However, they've made some mistakes in their lives and instead of the church loving them through their mistakes, we've judged them out of the church and out of The Word.

We've been so hard on them that they've doubled down on the enemy's way of thinking and decided that they won't marry according to God's plan, but according to their own time. Embraced by the world, we've lost them for a while.

If we could just learn to love people past our own perfections (let that sink in), we can turn them back to God's way of thinking. As for me,

I know I had to grow to marriage. I never resisted it, but I wasn't ready either. I still had some worldly ways to release before I was ready to be a husband.

Thankfully, in God's time, when I was ready, He sent my wife. But the battle I was initially fighting was within. The same is true with so many Christians that are resisting marriage these day.

What you want vs. what God orders

As we're growing towards marriage, this is really the first conflict we encounter. Long before we begin fighting with the opposite sex, we're fighting with ourselves and we're fighting with God.

We begin deciding what we want before even asking God to prepare us for marriage. More people are aware of what they're looking for long before they're aware of their needs. Choosing a mate must be done spiritually. Not doing so will ensure that we choose someone aesthetically pleasing, but not spiritually compatible.

We're initially in our flesh, so we'll initially try and satisfy our flesh. Who looks good on my arm? Who looks good in pictures with me? Who's so fine that people will be jealous of me? Who's gonna give me cute babies? And yes, we may as well keep it real, we as Christians wanna know, who's gonna look good in my bed?

All of these things that we want are often at the forefront of our thinking. So much so, that as we're chasing after our wants, we're running away from what God has planned for our lives.

Many of us, at one point or another in our lives, spent months, years, and maybe even decades chasing after someone that was far from what God wanted us to have. They may have been beautiful to us, or handsome, or doing well for themselves, and so on, but just because it's on the menu, that doesn't mean it's what God will order for you.

That's not all, however. There are also times when we're chasing someone that comes from good stock. Maybe they come from a good family with great values, with a solid foundation in The Lord, and appear to be a man or woman after God's own heart. But the fact still remains, what God has for you is for you.

Every good person that's available isn't necessarily for you. And even though they may have many of the qualities you're looking for, you'll find that if God didn't order it, you'll get together, but you won't necessarily click.

Try as you may to fit that square peg into that round hole, if God isn't in agreement, it won't last. Unequally yoked will always fall apart, even if it takes a long time.

Playing your position: Patience in the plan

As we're trying to navigate through those single days, we must surrender our will in favor of God's. I know it seems as if I'm suggesting that we shouldn't have a say in who we marry, and, well, I guess I am. I don't know about you, but I trust God's judgement over my own. His track record is spotless, and mine is, well, a lot less than perfect.

As a personal testimony, I dated a young lady off and on for years. I had told many that I loved her like a man loves his wife. Whenever we clashed, we forgave and we worked out our issues the way a married couple would. However, there were some personality clashes that we could never get past, and the things we couldn't get over were deal breakers for me.

God, in His infinite wisdom, knew that I would never marry her as long as these issues existed. I believe in my heart that every time I thought we had a chance, God caused a clash. He kept doing it until I left for good.

At that point, I stopped trying to force anything and I turned my search for a wife over to God. Once I saw what He had waiting for me, I knew within 10 minutes that she was the one. As much as I thought I loved someone else, God proved to me that I had a deeper love for who He would eventually send to be my helpmeet.

As a Christian, once you've been burned by your own wants a few times, you wind up asking God for guidance anyway. Just as we should when we pray for anything, we should be asking that God's will be done in our dating lives.

God is well aware of what we want for ourselves, and He's promised to give us the desires of our hearts. However, what we want for ourselves should line up with what God wants for us.

By having that first relationship that we should have, which is a relationship with God, we will be able to line up what we're looking for with what He would have for us.

I have to have enough faith in God and the fact that He loves me. I have to have enough Christian sense to know that He would only want me to have what's best for me, but He's going to give to me according to His purposes, not mine.

If I'm willing to pray to God with enough faith that He can handle my finances, I should have even more faith that He can choose a suitable mate for me. One that will satisfy every desire in my being.

A man should ask God to make him a suitable husband for one of His very best vessels. Before deciding what her dimensions should be, he should be more concerned with his spiritual dimensions.

Is he a suitable leader, protector, provider, father, and husband? Is he willing to follow God's lead so that the woman may feel comfortable following his? Before he even asks for a wife, he should be asking God to make him a husband. Not according to the standards of the world, but according to the standards of The Word.

A woman should be asking God to help her fulfill the edict of Proverbs 18:22, which tells her that she shouldn't be seeking a husband, he should be seeking her. Her role is to be in position to be found, for in finding her, the husband finds favor.

While she should keep herself up as best she can, she shouldn't be overly obsessed with her physical appearance because the man that God has prepared to find her will love her as she is, both physically and spiritually. God has changed this man's sight to vision and he sees her as God intends for him to see her, according to God's standards, and not the world's.

Before choosing a position, we must all learn to play the position that we're in. God has already planned all of this out. The only thing we can do by choosing on our own is prolong our destiny.

It takes a grcat deal of faith to allow someone else to choose the person that you'll spend the rest of your life with. It seems to me that we shouldn't be more willing to trust matchmaking sites or matchmaking friends before we trust the ultimate matchmaker in God.

Everybody submits!

If there's ever something that people struggle with as it relates to marriage, it has to be the idea of submission. Truthfully, this issue is more of a problem for women than it is for men, because when someone speaks the word "submit", many of us hear the word "slave".

Society has much to do with this as we've allowed worldly mindsets to enter into godly discussions. The world has sought to "empower" our women by telling them to never sacrifice their independence for anyone.

However, I'm still struggling to understand how the independent woman ever expects to be married. The idea of marriage is not only coming into agreement with another dependent party, but it's also to suggest that you need someone else for lifelong happiness. If that's not what the thinking is, why get married?

What I've found is that when you mention submission to a woman and she recoils in disgusts, she's either involved with a man that isn't worth that level of commitment, or a man like that is in her past.

If that's the case, that's not a reason to ignore God's command for submission. That's a reason for you to reconsider who you're involved with and make yourself available for God to upgrade your situation.

The mentality of the independent woman in this scenario is that she doesn't want to yield control. However, a complete understanding of Scripture and how God has designed marriage will show her that she's not yielding control to the man. She's yielding control to God.

The idea that God expects the woman to submit, but not the man, is false. The man is the first person that God expects to submit. Once the man submits to God, then the woman submits to the man, under God's leadership. God doesn't expect us to just blindly follow anyone, whether it be in marriage, church, or anywhere.

If we study Ephesians 5:22-33, we see God's plan. God wants a husband to love his wife just as Christ loves the church. When you consider what kind of love Christ has for the church (see Calvary), how could a woman not be willing and able to submit to a man with that much love for her?

This is one of the side effects of not doing marriage God's way. We date and "try things out" with people that we shouldn't even be mixing with, we have all of these bad experiences with the opposite sex, experiences that leave us so scarred and scared.

So when we finally come into the presence of Mr. or Mrs. Right, we struggle to follow God's command. This is how the enemy puts a struggle into the marriage before we even get to the altar.

Keeping the faith while dating

Speaking of the altar, how do we maintain our Christian focus on the way there? Christian dating is one the foremost challenges facing youth and young adults in the church today.

As a result of the rise of a come as you are culture in church, which is the way is which we should receive the lost, we've allowed them to stay as they came. We've sacrificed teaching God's way for fear that we may offend people or cause them to feel judged.

We must develop a way to reach our younger people, and some of the older ones that don't know better, without sacrificing the principles of Christianity. In regards to that, there are some expectations that God has for our dating lives.

As Christians in the dating world, we must be careful and cautious not to lay down our faith in order to pick up a mate. Those of us that are saved before marriage must understand that we will encounter people in the dating world that don't necessarily share in what we believe.

Many of them are saved as well, but they aren't necessarily living a saved lifestyle.

If you're on your way to the altar God-style, you must know that there are some restrictions on your behavior. As Christians, we shouldn't be looking to date just to mate as the world does. Our objective should be to marry.

I know that the world has updated what they do, and casual relationships along with casual sex is now the norm, but we're called to a higher standard in God. No matter how the world is getting together, we have to be different.

Now, as we've already discussed, men and women of God should be allowing Him to shape them so that they might be prepared to meet one another. That doesn't mean that dating is wrong. We don't have to rely on arranged marriages.

You've got to date people in order to get to know them. You've got to spend some time with people in order to see what it is that God has prepared for you. Christian dating is still possible, with Christian rules.

As a man that's made the mistakes of physical and sexual contact before marriage, I can tell you first hand that God didn't intend for us to go through all of the trials, setbacks, heartbreak, and difficulties that such actions cause.

When you consider all of the emotional baggage that we carry from relationship to relationship, all because we allowed the emotions we felt in the flesh to be heightened by the emotions that come with premarital sex, you've got to know that there was an easier way to get to where God wanted us to go.

The first thing to remember, whether man or woman, is that once you're saved, you belong to God. No matter what you did or how you lived before, once you've committed to God, you're His.

Understanding that means that to live according to the world's standards and not His is spiritual adultery. No matter what your body says, you must lean on your faith. You must stay faithful to God.

I know, it's easier said than done, and therein is the challenge for those of us that have already given in to the flesh. Once you have an appetite for something, it's hard to get the taste out of your mouth.

I know the world is telling us that it's easiest to try it before you buy it, but that's not God's way. Once you've experienced what God has waiting for you, you'll wonder why you ever tried anything else before.

Conversely, once you've wasted your time in places that He tried to keep you from, you may have learned a lesson, but what you've paid may be more than you really wanted to spend.

Run a red light, have an accident

One of the pitfalls of doing things man's way as opposed to God's is that we often create situations that make moving forward a challenge. Life doesn't become impossible, but it does become difficult. As much as God loves us, there must be consequences to our disobedience or we'll never do better.

As we discussed earlier, dating outside of The Word creates baggage, much of which is created by ignoring God's warning signs. And let's be honest here, when you're trying to get to your godly marriage, what you're carrying can be just as important as who you are as a person.

Not everyone is capable of dealing with someone with a past. Not everyone is capable of walking into a relationship where a child or children are already present. That's not said for anyone to be defensive. It's not said so that anyone can feel judged. It's a reality. These are facts.

Just as those of us that are carrying or have carried baggage have preferences, so to do those that are without those types of restrictions.

Understand what's being said here. There are no illegitimate children in God's sight, only illegitimate acts. The results are not the mistake, but the acts that bring them about are. If it were not so, there wouldn't be a proliferation of "baby mamas and baby daddies" around the world.

If mistakes aren't being made, there would be more organic families, and not as many blended families. God can bring blessings from all of these situations, but we must know that God turning a situation around doesn't mean that He approved of the direction that got us lost. Once we get Him involved, things improve.

The moment we begin doing things outside of God's original plan, we're doing things according to the plan of the enemy. The devil's plan is to destroy God's people though the lusts of their flesh.

All of the physical diseases we contract during sexual activity before marriage are not what God wanted for us (acknowledging that some disease comes from *within* the marriage; another book, another time). And even though children born under any circumstances are blessed of God and He still loves them, if they're born out of wedlock, they're a product of disobedience.

Even when we make children with those that God intended for us to be with, but we do it before the marriage, we're still out of order. Ending up in the right place doesn't absolve us of all of the wrong we do before get there. Only the blood of Jesus can absolve us.

Before anyone becomes confused, please understand what I'm saying: NEVER REGRET YOUR CHILDREN! Only regret disobeying God to get them. I was born out of wedlock and my first son was born out of wedlock, so I'm a witness that God won't throw you away, even if man wants to.

But I'm blessed that I have a mother that explained to me, as I did my oldest, that while there's no regretting the child, the action that leads to the unwedded birth is wrong in the sight of God.

So let's consider how many disastrous relationships we have with people that we have no business being with. Now, consider how many warning signs we had about that relationship along the way. Many of us pretend not to know how we wound up with certain individuals, when the truth of the matter is God always warns His children.

It may have been through advice from your parents, a warning from a friend, a sermon from the pastor, or the behavior of the individual that raised a flag.

I refuse to believe that God loves us enough to sacrifice His Son for our salvation, but He gave us no clue about the wrong person in our lives that we just fell into bed with. Even when we don't have foresight, we can always rely on His sight.

Again, we live and we learn, and I understand that. We are not our mistakes, and I understand that too. We don't have to carry it all because Jesus paid it all. All valid points.

However, we must stop using God only as a hero and start using Him as a protector. One who not only saves us from our mistakes, but also warns us before we make them.

We must begin using The Bible as our traffic light, telling us both when to go and when to stop. Experience is a great teacher, but contrary to popular belief, it's not the best teacher. God's Word is the best teacher.

Remember, it's not a race

Know that your path is just that, your path. The Word of God tells us that we have a race to run, and that applies to all things in our lives. Remember this as you date and long after you marry, there is no race being run except that of the individual.

So many of us feel as if we need to marry because someone else is getting married. Even after the marriages, we tend to measure our relationships against the relationships of others. Not only is this a good way to cause confusion in your household, but it's also a way to lose appreciation for what you've been blessed with.

One thing I've always been leery of is people that give marital advice based on their own relationship, without ever speaking to the couple they're advising to find out who they are and what works for them.

Whenever I advise couples on their relationship, I always start with God's Word. That's the standard. That's where it all begins for all people of the Christian faith. Whatever God says is for us, will work for us.

Beyond that, it comes down to the individual. The financial setup for my wife and I may not work for other couples. How we communicate is specific to us, and even if other couples admire it, the dynamic may not be what they're capable of.

At the same time, there may be others that we admire, but if we're not who they are, trying to do what they do may cause more friction than success.

Accepting that God has designed you and your mate for one another means accepting that you will have your own way about you. You'll have your own chemistry, your own languages, along with your own struggles that only the two of you can help one another through.

It's good to admire those that have successful relationships, and even to allow them to mentor you in some aspects. But it's most important to make your own lane and do what works for you. Run YOUR race, but you're not in competition with anyone.

Trouble in paradise

There's no doubt that marriage comes with good days and challenging days. How we handle adversity determines whether or not we will succeed.

There are some that believe that if there isn't an argument or two in a relationship, there's no real passion. I contend that embracing arguments as necessary to the spark of your relationship is like playing with fire. Sooner or later, you're going to go to a place that you can't quite get back from.

Fighting isn't a way to show love to your partner, it's a way to show love to your position. I believe people ought to fight *for* their marriages, but not within their marriages.

There should always be room for healthy disagreement, as no two people will always see eye to eye, but there is a difference between a disagreement and an argument. One is constructive, and one can be destructive. There will be enough people for the two of you to take on together concerning your marriage without the two of you battling each other.

Speaking of which, we must guard our marriages against attacks from the enemy. Outside of arguments disguised as "sparks" or "passion", people from outside your relationship will attempt to tear it apart. There's jealousy, hatred, and quite honestly, some people that just don't wanna see you or anyone else happy.

The Bible tells us that when a man and a woman are joined together in matrimony, the two become one flesh (Matthew 19:5). What God is trying to stress to us is that the marriage is one unit. We are no longer separate, but we are one. This is why the arguing makes no sense. You're literally arguing within our own body.

Just imagine what would happen to you if your kidneys and your liver were in disagreement. Imagine what would happen if your heart refused to pump blood to the rest of your body. This is what it's like when there's a war within a singular flesh. No matter how strong you think you are, the body begins to fail.

At the same time, when you allow outside forces into the body, it will cause sickness, and some sickness can lead to death. Once we're married, we must be mindful of who we bring around the body because of the disease they carry.

You must know that whom you considered friend *before* the marriage may not be a friend *of* the marriage. Again, some people aren't happy that you've found someone. For all that you feel you're gaining, they may feel that they're losing. You can't let that damage what God has given you.

Another challenge marriages face is people that will only like one half of the whole. But any friend that isn't a friend of the entire body isn't a friend of the marriage. My position is that you can't love me and hate my wife. She is a part of me, and many married couples need to learn to see their marriages this way.

If you're truly operating as one flesh, as God has ordered you, there are no more individual friends. Even if we don't all hang out together, you must be a friend of the marriage, which means you can't hate or even dislike the other half of me.

If you consume something that doesn't agree with part of your body, it effects the whole body. I've often told my wife that if someone hugs her, but won't even speak to me, they don't mean either of us any good. That kind of thing only serves as a source of confusion, division, and a potential argument within the marriage.

Why did you embrace them when you know they don't like me? Are you cosigning their negative feelings about me? Are they talking about me to you? This all seems insecure, but those are questions we'd ask any friend hugging a sworn enemy, right? Don't think it won't happen in a marriage.

In this situation, a person needs to be told, "If you have a problem with my spouse, you have one with me". Require that it's worked out so that there doesn't appear to be a divide in your marriage.

The Bible tells us to avoid the appearance of evil (1 Thessalonians 5:22), so it does matter what it looks like. If your partner feels some kind of way about a relationship that you have, it's your job to put them at ease. Even in the case of an insecure partner, your job is to make them feel secure.

Solid marriages built on God's Word, love, trust, and communication can survive anything sent their way. No marriage is devoid of bad days, disagreements, and misunderstandings. It's how you handle all of those things that will determine your success.

Keeping God at the center is the key to it all. Being mindful that we're all capable of being wrong helps as well. Above all, remember that forgiveness begins with an apology. Don't look to be right, look to get it right.

What God has broken apart...

As much as we all want our relationships to work, we must realize that sometimes, they don't. There are times when God ordered a marriage, but the participants decide against what God ordered and become self-destructive.

However, most breakups come when people tried to force something that God was against. But God is not a liar. If He's against what you're doing, you'll never be successful. Even if you try and hold it together, if God says no, it will end.

In the case of what's failing, in the midst of all of the pain and heartache that it may cause, we must learn to trust God. Sometimes He's just pulling you out of a dead situation.

We talked earlier about running the red lights that God places in our lives, and heartbreak and wasted years are often the consequences of our disobedience. Often we feel as if people changed on us, and that may be the case, especially when people get married young. But there are times when they didn't necessarily change, but rather they grew into who they were going to be in life.

There is a maturation process that we all go through, and sometimes we've connected with people when they weren't quite done growing. We fell in love with who they were, but once they became who they were going to be, the fairy tale ended.

But then, there are those times when we blinded ourselves, pretending that people are who we wanted them to be, when the truth of the matter is they were never any of that and the signs were everywhere. We ran the red light and collided with reality.

Nobody likes a breakup but they are a part of life for many of us. All of us weren't blessed enough to meet the love of our lives in high school, get married and stay together for 50 years. Many of us, through our own doing, will have that trial and error experience.

Just remember, when things fall apart, let God heal your heart. Don't try and get back out there too soon. Don't try and put a band aid on a massive wound. When we breakup, we're often embarrassed. So much so, that we want to get back out there as soon as possible. Not just to prove to others that we aren't hurt, but to prove it to ourselves.

After a breakup, there is a healing process and we must go through it. Believe me, just because we chose against God's wishes doesn't mean He won't bring us back to good mental and spiritual health.

When I wrote my first book, *Temporarily Disconnected*, I detailed a very painful breakup that I went through. Had my heart broken and everything. One of the things I did was take my time.

I didn't determine how long I should be down or when I should love again, nor did I operate based on how long someone else thought I should be out of commission. I trusted God with the healing.

What I learned is that we have no control over when we'll be over. It sounds really cliché, but we really do have to take it one day at a time.

Some days will be good days, and some not so good.

If you decide how long the healing is supposed to take, if you end up wrong, now you've added more anger and frustration to your pain. The key is not micromanaging God. Don't tell Him how long it should take Him to heal your heart. Just trust Him to do it in His own time.

Marriage still matters: Minister to someone!

More than anything, I'd like to stress that marriage is a ministry. God ordained marriage and He blessed it. We must use our marriages to encourage others. We must use our marriages as something that people can look forward to in their lives. Not to mimic what we have, but rather to aspire to the happiness that we have.

Each marriage is unique and that in itself is a blessing. My wife and I have something that no one else has and it's tailored just for us. We do our best to be an example of what God had in mind for marriage.

In our best moments, we're loving one another. In the very, very few moments when we disagree, we're loving each other through it. Just as God requires reconciliation in our relationships with our fellow man, He requires the same thing within the marriage.

For Valentine's Day, I posted this of my wife on social media:

"There could be no one for me but you. When all of the cards are against me, I'm still holding a Queen. Loving you is as natural as breathing. Happy Valentine's Day to my year 'round love. May we always share a love that makes God so proud, that He brags on us for honoring Him."

The point of the post is that we want to be an example of what it is God intended. I once wrote an article for a relationship site where I discussed the divorce rate in America, which at the time was about 50%.

However, I wanted to write about how the other half lived. We often focus so much on failing marriages that those that are successful get swept under the rug. We need to make an effort to let the world know that real and enduring marriages still exist.

I have several friends in the ministry that are successfully married. That's not to suggest that only ministers can be successful in marriage because there are some that make the same mistakes that others make, and their marriages fall apart. I'm simply stating that men and women of God are still forming life-long bonds, and they're still doing it according to God's Word. We need to celebrate that.

I've counseled young couples that have had the sincerest desire to be married. They believe in the institution that God ordained. This is encouraging and I'm always honored to be asked to assist someone in holding on to love.

In a world where marriage God's way is being seen as outdated, we must encourage as many as we can to be what God wants them to be, and not what the world is willing to accept.

Let us continue to carry the ministry of marriage forward for a new generation of believers, who's secular idols tells them that a piece of paper doesn't make a difference. We must remind them that the Word of God is still true when it says that marriage is honorable. It's not just about a "piece of paper". Marriage is more than any document.

The marriage is represented in how the two become one and live as God has ordered. As I stated in the very first marriage ceremony I officiated: "The ceremony is how the public knows you're married, the license is how the state knows your married, but the relationship is how God knows you're married".

Chapter 4

Going from death to life

One of the most difficult things any of us will go through in life is the death of a loved one. No matter what your level of faith is, when death strikes, it can cripple you physically, emotionally, and spiritually.

A personal relationship with God doesn't exempt one from the pain of mama or grandma dying. In fact, it is often our faith that brings more questions:

- Why me God, when I serve You so diligently?
- Why my loved one when *they* served You so diligently?
- I'm saved, why do I feel just as much pain after loss as the unsaved?

In the case of an unnatural or violent death:

- Why did they have to die like *that*, Lord?

And, believe it or not, this is a common question asked by those that are saved:

- How do I go on from here?

While we know that God hears all of these questions and concerns when we're in a state of bereavement, knowing that He hears them and not always receiving the response we want to hear at that time can be of little consolation.

Depending on who just died, we often feel like dying ourselves. But know that it's not the will of God for us to die when He calls someone else home. It is God's will that we live on until He calls us home.

In order for us to go from the death of a loved one to living again, we must come to understand death itself in the best way that we can. One of the things that we don't do enough of in the church is teaching on physical death. We talk much of Jesus' death, burial, and resurrection, but we don't talk about the physical death of the saved and the spiritual resurrection that is to come.

The most we ever talk about it is during a funeral, where attention spans and understanding are at their lowest. Don't misunderstand me, if there's ever a time to talk about eternal life, it's during a eulogy when mortality is on everyone's mind. However, I believe that we can do a better job of preparing the saints for the inevitability of death while they are yet reasonably healthy and living their lives.

The lessons of mortality

"For man also does not know his time: Like fish taken in a cruel net, like birds caught in a snare, so the sons of men are snared in an evil time, when it falls suddenly upon them." – Ecclesiastes 9:12 (NKJV)

The loss of any life is a warning to those of us that remain. When considering death, we must understand that God has many different lessons for us to learn. One being that even when we're alive, but in sickness, we're still blessed.

We may not be feeling our best, but somebody's not feeling at all. We can't lose faith because we're struggling physically. God is a wonderful God, in sickness and in health. If you don't believe me, ask somebody that the doctor gave up on, but God made a way.

Understanding that death is final, let's look at a few things we should consider when facing the death of a loved one:

Death reminds us of our own mortality – I've always taught that 30 is what I call the first age of reflection. It is the first time in which we take inventory of our lives and the choices that we've made to that point. That's the age that we all expect to have certain milestones in life passed. Career, marriage, house, children, and financial stability.

However, what makes it a much more important milestone than other ages like 16, 18, and 21, is when we reach 30 and begin taking inventory of our lives, we also realize that we're going to die one day. All of the things we look at when turning 30 are related to our legacy. We finally realize that we're not invincible and that we will in fact die.

However, nothing brings mortality to the forefront of our minds like the death of a loved one. More so than the death of an acquaintance or someone we barely know, the death of a loved one and the emotion that comes with it puts it squarely in our minds that our day is coming too. We often become reflective, just as we do at age 30, about what we've done with our lives. We understand that there's a graveyard in everyone's path, and we're not exempt.

Death reminds us that our time is limited – An unexpected death teaches us that we don't always have as much time as we think we do. If it were up to us, we'd all have long, healthy lives. We think that, in spite of the fact that scripture tells us that we're only here for a few days, and those days are full of trouble (Job 14:1).

At the funeral of someone that died suddenly, you're likely to hear two statements being made: "Gone too soon" or "God doesn't make any mistakes".

Let's deal with the first statement. While teaching Bible class to a group of young people, I asked this question: How much time does God give us? It's a question that many don't think about. Scripture tells us threescore and 10 years (70), and if by reason of strength, we may get fourscore (80) (Psalms 90:10).

But we all know someone that died long before that age, right? Death can be so sudden and so unpredictable, how can anyone really answer the question of how much time God gives? My answer to them was "God gives us just as much time as we need".

That leads us to that second statement, "God doesn't make any mistakes". As we're in the midst of death, it's easy to believe that God got it wrong because He went against our wishes. In fact, that emotion is understandable. But a true awareness of God and His infinite wisdom can keep us from believing in that emotion while we're in a moment of anger, frustration, and bereavement.

He gives us all the days we need to do whatever He has purposed us to do. It is true, God doesn't make any mistakes, and for that reason, nobody goes too soon. He's just too wise to make a mistake.

This doesn't mean that we don't get to ask God why. I don't believe God doesn't want to be questioned, but we should never do so as if

He's wrong. We should only ask for understanding. In time, He may answer and He may not. But one thing is for sure, He will comfort those that allow Him to.

If we don't get anything else out of sudden death, we should get the fact that tomorrow is in fact not a guarantee. Our time is limited and we aren't all given the same amount.

I've been on program at funerals for someone in their seventies as well as a 4 month old child. While I don't understand God's choices in death and I dare not try to explain them, I do believe that all lives have purpose, and all deaths have a lesson somewhere.

Death reminds us of the preciousness of life on both sides of the grave – From the moment we're conceived in our mother's womb, we're dying. Even as we grow and grow, we're actually growing ever closer to the grave.

As we're reminded that death isn't reserved for the old and can come upon any of us suddenly, we must take inventory of how we live from day to day. There's so much that we take for granted without realizing that in an instant, either we or someone that we care about can be gone.

Something we often put on the back burner is our relationship with God. But living a saved life isn't something that we should be reserving for later in life. Salvation is a precious gift, given to us by God. We must take advantage as soon as possible.

Scripture tells us to remember our Creator in the days of our youth (Ecclesiastes 12:1). God can use you at any stage in life, but he does want you young and vibrant.

Understand that God doesn't want us to live our lives looking over our shoulders. He expects us to enjoy ourselves. However, there are some things that we put off doing because we're in good health, or we're young, or the people in our families usually live a long time.

Time we could be spending with those we care about easily turns into time wasted with disingenuous people that we're trying to impress.

We're holding grudges and withholding forgiveness, when we could be enjoying life with loved ones and putting bitterness aside. Sometimes people die and there are unresolved issues. There are relationships that weren't what they should've been. Things that weren't settled before the end. Stuff that causes great amounts of grief.

These are the things that tear us apart at the funeral. All of the coulda, woulda, shoulda's. All the things we regret not doing because we thought we had time that we didn't have. Life is precious and should be treated as such, and it shouldn't always take death for us to realize that.

Additionally, as we live our lives here on earth, we should do so with an eye towards life beyond the grave. Instead of trying our best to hold on to this earthly life, we should always be looking to gain Heaven. We should always be looking for life eternal.

While salvation is offered to all, many haven't taken advantage. That life eternal that Jesus died for is our reward. Heaven is our final resting place. Knowing that life is fleeting should cause us to want to do better and be better to one another. Goodbyes won't be so

---

hard if we'd just appreciate the gift of the lives we have with each other.

Death is actually a sign of new beginnings – I know this isn't on our minds at the funeral home or in church at the home going service, but give it some thought. As for the dead in Christ, this is the end of an earthly life, but the beginning of an everlasting life with Christ.

As for those of us that are still here, an earthly legacy must be taken over. It is the beginning of many of us learning that God is in fact a comforter.

Many are standing in the funeral home claiming that they don't know how they'll go on from that moment. But in the coming days, months, years, and in some cases, decades, they will find that God is a keeper and that if they allow Him, He'll turn incredible sadness into sweet, sweet memories.

While death can be contentious in some families due to a myriad of circumstances, in stronger family units, there are three things that the unpredictability of death can bring: Forgiveness, repentance, and reconciliation. The truth is sometimes it takes a death for us to realize just how petty some arguments are, how silly the grudges are, and the fact that we really and truly love one another.

I have a testimony

In March of 2012, we lost my niece Olivia at the age of 18. She was in her first year of college and her future was extremely bright. Her death was sudden and not what any of us expected. It literally tore my family apart emotionally because she was truly everyone's shining star.

I've never met a soul that didn't absolutely adore her. When a presence like that is taken away, even the strongest of Christians will look to the sky and wonder who's making the decisions. It never seemed fair that Olivia, of all people, would only have 18 years.

Outside of secular accomplishments, Olivia loved The Lord with a passion. She was involved in everything that a child could possibly be involved in concerning church. As I wrote in her obituary, she was the best student in the youth Bible class I taught. I actually give her some of the credit for molding me into the teacher I am today because she asked so many questions and I wanted to make sure she had all of the answers she was seeking.

I wrote of her in a weekly email that I used to do that she lived the best 18 years of life I had ever seen. I know she wasn't perfect, but she was perfectly Olivia and I've never met a child so warm and so loving. I'm blessed to have been connected to her, but as devastating as her death was in my family, it was only the tip of the iceberg for a very difficult spring to come.

As we were still reeling from my niece's death, just a few weeks later in early April, my Uncle Dan passed. He wasn't just my uncle, he was also my spiritual father and the pastor of our church for 23 years. The contrast of death was so evident, as Olivia died at 18 and Uncle Dan at age 81.

This was the man that was most instrumental in shaping and molding me into the teacher, and eventually preacher, that I am today (although he would pass away before I preached my first sermon, he had already told me what God had revealed to him concerning my ministry).

A pillar of spiritual strength in our family, this was a crushing blow. It seemed as if God had come to get two of our most spiritual family members. Within a matter of weeks, I lost my best student and my teacher. My favorite niece and my favorite uncle. Although my faith remained strong, my strength was waning.

Determined to pick up the mantle that my uncle had dropped on me, I vowed to journey on anyway. But God wasn't done. The following month in May, on Mother's Day, my wife's grandmother passed away. No one knew just how sick she was, so this death came out of the blue as well.

So not only was my biological family reeling, but now, so was my wife's family. This really hit my wife hard because she was so close to her grandmother, so my personal grief was interrupted so that I could grieve with my wife, while doing my duty in care for her.

As we returned from California and the funeral of our dearly departed, we were hoping to get back to some sort of normalcy. But God was not yet done with me or my family. Later in that same month, I lost another uncle. This was my mother's oldest brother and it left her without any living siblings.

I had no time to break down at all because I had to be strong for my mom. With my nephew having died the previous year in August, in less than a year, my mom had lost two grandchildren and two brothers. If there had ever been a family that was being tested by death, our family was the one.

After rolling in and out of funeral homes month after month, you would think that my family would've been ready to give up on life. And we weren't dealing with the deaths of distant relatives and casual acquaintances. These were people that were close to us.

The easiest thing to do would've been to wallow in self-pity, accuse God of being unfair, and lose our faith, and I can't tell you that no one in my family didn't do just that. There are many of us that are still struggling to this very day. But whenever someone in the family would ask me why this kept happening to us, my response was always "Why everyone else and not us?"

If you turn on the news, there comes a point where you see a family that's lost a loved one, and sometimes in the interview, you'll find out that they had another death a short time before.

Again, I don't claim to know why God does what He does, but sometimes death comes in two's and three's. How can I question the fairness of God if what happens to others can and did actually happen to me?

Is everyone else's grandma supposed to die, but not mine? Are everyone else's loved ones supposed to leave sooner than they thought, but not mine because I'm saved? How many people have someone in their families that won't die?

Death is a part of life and everyone has their turn. It doesn't make us cold to accept this fact, it just means that we're grounded in reality, even when we're filled with grief. No one likes to deal with tragedy, particularly back to back, but it is a part of life. Today it may be someone else's time, tomorrow it may be yours, and the next day belongs to someone else.

In the midst of death, those of us in the faith understand that there's always a silver lining somewhere. It's just hard to see through the tears. Many of us know that there are better days ahead, but it's hard to accept that in the midst of the frustration.

We know that God knows best, but it's hard to accept that when you're so angry, both at the situations, and quite honestly, at God. However, if we just trust Him, we will begin to see His power.

***

In the midst of all that my family had gone through, we were still able to see God's glory. Shortly before Olivia passed, my wife and I had found out that she was pregnant with our first child together.

While it was a struggle with her carrying a child while going through so much grief, that baby boy growing inside her was a bright light at the end of a very long and dark tunnel.

I often told her that there was going to be something special about him. Not because he was ours, but because of what God had taken us through. We had suffered so much with all of that death, and I believed that the life that

God had growing inside her was going to be the boost that this family needed. And Kilen didn't disappoint.

With all that we had been through in death, it seemed as if my entire family was looking forward to my son with anticipation. When he showed up that fall, it actually seemed to create a bond in the family.

And to show just how awesome God is, He answered my prayers by sending Kilen on Uncle Dan's birthday, about 2 ½ weeks before he was actually due. After what we went through that spring, by fall, God showed that He was still a God that will bring life when situations seem hopeless.

Kilen is a most special child. Very intelligent at 3 years of age, very musical, and very engaging. As if God's hand isn't enough there, he seems to be carrying the spirit of both Olivia and Uncle Dan.

He has Olivia's smarts and engaging personality, while being quite spiritual like Uncle Dan, having been able to pray since he was 2, and with a love for praising God. If there was a moment that we questioned God with all of the death we saw, we had to praise God for the life He sent.

So, how do we get up?

Something that I always say whenever I'm asked to preach at a funeral or give remarks is God doesn't intend for us to stay at the funeral home or the cemetery.

Too often, we commemorate the death of our loved ones by mourning *continuously*. When their birthdays come around, we get together, not to celebrate, but to mourn.

We wear t-shirts that constantly remind us that they died, but not t-shirts that show the joy in which they lived. We have become a society of mourners that fail to embrace the good times we had with a lost loved one.

We fail to remember that we all have an earthly expiration date. Even if we don't understand death in the moment, particularly when it's sudden, unexpected, or tragic, we must remember that tomorrow is promised to no one. We're all going to die, and while we don't always know why, we must understand that it is a reality.

Believe it or not, understanding and embracing the inevitability of all people dying can and will help us in getting through it. As long as something feels impossible or improbable, it becomes harder to take when the impossible and improbable comes to pass.

That mindset won't eliminate the question of "why" that comes, and Lord knows that we don't always like the "how". But if we start with the understanding that it can and will happen to all of us, we're not in the funeral home and the church with the emotions of someone that feels they're mourning someone that was once thought to be indestructible.

Embracing the idea of death doesn't endear us to people dying. It doesn't bring us to a happy place, as we're knowing that in order to see our loved one again, we too have to die. However, it does help to prepare us for the inevitable.

Once we've been struck down by death, getting up is the thing that's most difficult. The questions I hear most often are: "What am I gonna do?" and "How am I gonna go on?" We as Christians must understand that no matter how we feel, we are not alone in this thing. We have to understand that getting through death requires someone strong enough to help us through.

There may be friends, family, and churches that can help us to get through, but the reality is only God can get us up from such a devastating life event. But here's the catch: He can only get you up if you trust Him, and if you let Him.

The only death that would've been eternally catastrophic for man would've been the death of Jesus Christ. But we know that Christ is no longer in the grave, so we still have hope. This is why God doesn't want us perpetually mourning in the cemeteries.

When they went to the tomb looking for Jesus, they were told He was not there. He had risen! And because Jesus got up, no death here on earth is final for those that believed on Him. Because Jesus is alive, no Christian should ever have the mindset that they can't go on. In times of earthly death, we must remember the life of Jesus because it's going on to this very day.

Sometimes the greatest test of our faith is in death. Losing someone that's close to you, that you cared for deeply, can cause you to want to die. We have to keep our faith in a living God.

People will say that they can't make it without a certain individual, but as long as they don't terminate their own lives, you'll look up and 5, 10, 15, 20 years later, and they're still carrying on. Only God can do that.

Thoughts turn to the fact that we'll never be the same because of a death, and people that feel that way are absolutely right. People that you love shouldn't leave your life and you go back to normal.

You should be changed. You should be different. And if you allow God to do the healing, you'll find that one of the most significant things that will change about you is your level of faith, because He helped you to carry on when you thought you couldn't.

For someone that seems intent on mourning, you might read these words and say that I've oversimplified the mourning process. You may feel that I've made something very difficult seem very simple, when it's not really that easy.

You may even say that I don't understand. However, I would have you to go back and re-read those paragraphs on my 2012 spring. If that isn't enough, I lost my big brother when I was 20.

I've lost grandmothers. I've lost childhood friends, both as a child, and as an adult. I've seen tragic deaths in my family as well as slow deaths. But I promise you, I still have my joy because through it all, God still kept me.

I had moments when I didn't think I could go on, and I had moments when it all seemed unfair, as if God was picking on me, but I see now that He was preparing me. There's no way I could tell you how faith will bring you through if I didn't know from personal experience.

I despise death just as much as anyone reading these words, but I promise you that I'm better able to handle it now because God has always brought the sunshine back to my life.

I still cry when people die, I still have my time to mourn, and certain deaths take longer than others to get over, but I know that God is a healer because He healed my heart every time, and He can do the same for others if they'd only trust Him.

∗∗∗

The human struggle is that we don't like the idea of anything being beyond our control. This is why going from death to life is so difficult. We're saved, but we don't always fully understand that in order to live forever with Christ, we must leave here.

We wanna be safe in His arms, but that requires a transition. Not just for you, but for your loved ones as well. However, the only time we should mourn with a sense of hopelessness is when someone that wasn't saved dies because we know that there is no salvation.

Jesus conquered death, so we as Christians don't have to worry about our souls. Therefore, we shouldn't concern ourselves with our bodies. Once we come to understand that we are in fact spirits with bodies and not the other way around, we'll come to the realization that we will live on in Jesus, even after this body has worn out and given up the ghost.

If we can understand that fact for our own lives, how much better would we understand that for the lives of our saved loved ones when they transition?

Going from death to life is understanding that this earth is not our permanent dwelling place. It's understanding that God holds it all in His hands. What we may lose in the physical presence of a loved one gone, we gain in the spiritual presence of God as He wraps His arms around us during times of bereavement.

What we must learn to do is embrace the good times and good memories. Even when someone dies and the relationship wasn't the best, God can fix that too if we give Him the chance and give Him the time.

Here's the key: Healing isn't instant, but it comes in time. Grief doesn't come with an "in" door only. There is a way out and that way is through Jesus. When we just let Him work, sooner or later, we start to feel better after deaths.

Don't fight that feeling. Don't feel guilty about smiling again. Don't feel bad about life returning to some sense of normalcy. That's a trick of the enemy, as he wants you constantly in a state of mourning, doubting that God can ever heal your heart.

When you start to feel better, God is answering your prayers. You asked to get through it, and He's delivering you. You asked to be able to sleep at night, and He's giving you rest. You asked to smile again, and He's giving you a reason to. When He's healing you, take the medicine.

There's much more of life to live. Don't carry the graveyard with you for the rest of your life. Carry God's healing. Carry the good times. Carry the laughs. Carry the joy. Most of all, carry that everlasting bond that's still there. Because it never existed body to body. It existed spirit to spirit.

Chapter 5

The ministry of life: Faith, finance, and applying God's Word

You can't effectively exercise faith in something that you're unsure about. Many Christians struggle in their faith because they not only aren't really sure about who God is, but they've blindly ignored all that He's already done in their lives. This is common because we tend to focus on the few things in life that have gone wrong without remembering all of the many things that have gone right.

Our religion is built on faith in God, His promises, and the fact that Jesus was born of a virgin in the flesh, died on the cross, and rose again on the third day with all power in His hands.

Now, that was simply stated, but how many of us as Christians really and truly believe it? How many of us really understand that only a God without limits could do something so miraculous? How many of us have really accessed what it takes to believe what we claim to? How many of us have actually taken that leap of faith?

The truth of the matter is we've confused church attendance with some level of faith. We've confused church membership with some level of faith. However, the moment something doesn't go as we planned within the church walls, we assume that God has lost control. The moment the devil seems to be having his way in our lives, we act as if he's overpowered God.

We must remember that faith can't just be spoken. It must be exercised. Not during good times, because everything's alright then. It's during the bad times that we must exercise our faith.

During those times when we can't see our way out. During those times when the marriage is a struggle, when the kids are disobedient, when the church is falling apart, and when the family doesn't seem fractured, but broken instead. Those are the times when we must call on our faith in God, but you can't call on something that you don't understand or believe in.

In my book *An Understanding with God*, I listed some attributes of God and why we should trust Him. I discussed the fact that we often fail to trust God because He hasn't told us exactly how He's going to work it out. Because we haven't seen the blueprints, we don't trust the plans.

We often throw around the fact that we're blessed and highly favored when things are going well, but when things aren't their best, we struggle to believe that God can turn it around.

As Christians that believe in Calvary's cross, it amazes me that we don't quite believe that God can handle the day-to-day struggles that we face. I can assure you that my faith has increased, not only because of all that God has brought me through, but because of what I've seen Him do in the lives of others.

From the stories of The Bible to the stories of friends, family, associates, and even enemies, I've seen God's hand do remarkable things. This is what sustains me during the rough times, this is what encourages me when it seems as if the enemy won't let up, and this is what keeps me sane when I feel as if everyone has abandoned me.

***

"20 Now unto Him that is able to do exceeding abundantly above all that we ask or think, according to the power that worketh in us,

21 *Unto Him be glory in the church by Christ Jesus throughout all ages, world without end. Amen." – Ephesians 3:20-21 (KJV)*

To serve a God that you didn't really and truly believe could do all the things stated in that verse above would be the equivalent of serving man as though he is God. And while that Verse does acknowledge a power that's working in us, what we believe starts with God and His capabilities.

If we don't believe that He can do what His Word says He can do, we're in a vulnerable state. Not because He's not capable, but because we don't believe He's capable. If you don't believe that God can make a way, you're more likely to give up on the way.

When Job was going through his trial and he got angry, God confronted him. When God went to explain to Job how great He was (Job Chapters 38 and 39), He used examples of things that we take for granted. "Simple" things like who hung the stars in the sky and parted the seas, things we take for granted, God questioned Job about.

In those Chapters, God explained how complicated these "simplicities" of life really are, and that no one but God Himself could've done them. If you don't know just how awesome God is, you'll have no idea why you should trust Him beyond what your eyes can see and your mind can understand.

What's done in the spirit is often misunderstood by the flesh. As we seek to strengthen our faith, we can and will be weakened by our flesh if we allow it. The impossibilities of life become possible when we see things as God has called us to see them, in the spirit.

As life continues to challenges us, it's faith that helps us to win. It's faith that helps us to understand that even when we appear to lose, that God is still in control and the outcome is always by His design and for His purposes.

Something that I often state in relation to entrepreneurship is that the people closest to us struggle to support us because as humans, we like finished products, not works in progress. Nobody wants to be on the ground floor of what you're building, but they'll show up once the elevators to the top floor are installed.

Faith is like that in the sense that we sometimes don't want to work with God *through* anything. We want the victory without the hard work of practice and preparation. We want the progress without the process.

Again, we're fleshly and secular in our thinking. We wouldn't work a job for two weeks without knowing what the paycheck is gonna look like, and so we don't wanna put our faith where our mouth has been unless God tells us exactly how it's gonna turn out.

It seems to me that faith should be the one thing that we wouldn't wanna be lacking as Christians. We carry so much in the way of burdens that we sometimes don't feel as if we can survive. But I'm telling you, as much as we try to pick up and carry on our own, if we'd just add faith to the load that we're already carrying, we'd find that the load would get lighter.

We'd find that trials, though difficult, won't destroy us. We'd find that God is in fact with us. Shaping us, molding us, and preparing us for the long haul of life. All we have to do is keep the faith.

Christian crisis control: Who says God won't put more on you than you can bear?

If we never needed God's help with anything, we'd never need God. That seems simple enough to understand. The times we understand this need the most is during times of crisis. When life is spinning out of control, often the first thing to come from our mouths are the words "Lord, have mercy".

There's a thought that's been circulating throughout Christian circles for years and years. Here it is: "God won't put more on you than you can bear".

We've all heard it, and the vast majority of us have used it. The idea is to remind us that even in our most difficult struggles, God cares enough not to really cripple us, even though that's how we feel at certain times.

Also, the idea is to let us know that we're stronger than we think we are, and God knows our limits. On the surface, it's really an uplifting statement that says "You can make". However, at its core, in my opinion, it's incorrect.

As we discuss this as Christian crisis control, this statement seems to be preparing us for a life without God. I know that seemed like a wrong statement to make, but bear with me.

If God only gives me what I can handle on my own, then why would I ever pray that prayer "Lord, have mercy"? Why would such a prayer even exist? Why would I be calling on God to help me with what I can handle?

Understand what I'm saying here. In my opinion, the statement "God wouldn't put more on you than you can bear" would be better served if we said it in relation to blessings or an anointing.

For example, God may anoint you for a task that you don't feel you're capable of performing, but because of how He has prepared you, you're more capable than you know.

That's not to suggest that you go forward without God, but it is to suggest that God has purposed you and made you ready for your assignment. He won't give you what He hasn't enabled you to handle. Your prayer life, your obedience, and your sacrifice has made you ready in the sight of The Lord, and He will help you to maintain what you carry.

Where this statement falls short is during times of crisis. As previously stated, when God prepares you for a blessing, if you stay in His will, He will help you to keep it. But who can be prepared for the news that you've got cancer? Who can be prepared for the sudden death of a loved one?

Who can be prepared for the unexpected loss of a job and long term unemployment when you've got a family to provide for? Who's really ready for wayward children or a broken marriage? And if these were things that we could all handle, why do they damage us so?

We referenced the story of Job earlier, and when you consider what he went through in just one day, I imagine it crushed him, even though Scripture says that he never charged God foolishly (Job 1:22).

The truth of the matter is God puts things on us all the time that we can't bear. How else can you explain the pain of a mother standing over the casket of her child having never made it past the age of 16? Are we ready to believe that a person can bear such a tragedy alone?

That statement is really a way to encourage someone and to let them know that they'll make it through a difficult time in life. But if we really examine what we're saying, aren't we really just telling someone to toughen up, when they just wanna fall apart?

Isn't this telling someone to stop crying, while maybe not fully understanding their level of pain? The truth is we all process differently. What you may be able to carry could be an unbearable load to someone else. By encouraging people to carry pain on their own because they're "built for this" or they can "handle it", we're actually causing unnecessary strain.

Think of what it's like on your body when you carry things for too long. You may have started out handling it well, but as time goes on and you carry it for long enough, even what's light begins to feel heavy. The idea that we were meant to carry all of the burdens of life on our own is not only a lonely idea, it's not a godly idea.

When we're telling our brothers and sisters that they can handle it during times of crisis, we're crippling them emotionally, and sometimes physically. Instead of telling them what God wouldn't do in the way of putting things on them, we need to tell them what God can do in the way of lifting burdens and lightening the load.

We need to remind them that God does not exist to weigh us down with problems and tell us to carry them or else. No, in fact, when we're weighed down with the tragedies of life, God wants us to call on Him so that He can be that ever present help that He promised to be.

***

God puts things on us all the time that we can't bear, but it wasn't His original design. Because of the presence of sin in the world, we have trials and tribulations. We have death, painful births, tilling of the ground, the presence of evil, and so on. All things that we're not equipped to handle all the time and on our own.

If we'd just study our Bibles a little more, we'd find story after story of man crying out to God in times of trouble, and God in fact showing up. Never did He forsake us with a simple "You got this".

We sometimes don't understand that the fairness of God isn't in the equal distribution of blessings, but rather in the fact that all the blessings don't belong to one person, but neither do all of the tragedies.

We all have to go through something, and there are times when what you're going through will be more than you alone can bear. As my uncle, the late Pastor Dan Flowers used to say, "God may put a load on you, but He won't put an overload on you". I interpreted that to mean that God won't try and kill you with a burden, but we all have some burdens to bear.

Don't misunderstand this discourse. The more God takes us through, the more we're equipped to handle certain trials in life. In fact, we're even able to testify to others, encourage them, and strengthen them.

However, there will always be that "Lord, have mercy" moment. There will always be a time when we call on God because He's the only one that can carry us through.

No matter who you are in this life, you've faced a moment or two when neither friends, family, pastor, nor church members can help you through. You can call on no one but God to deliver you.

In our darkest hours and our most critical moments, we need to go to God in prayer because that's where the answer is. That's where the relief is. That's where the healing is.

We never get stuck in moments like this because God has left us. We get stuck in moments like this because we sometimes believe that we can carry things on our own.

This is why we'd be better served to tell people the truth of God's power. "God will come to your rescue", which is the truth, seems to be a much more uplifting sentiment than "God put this on you, so you'll just have to carry it".

When the Apostle Paul pleads with God to remove the thorn from His flesh (2 Corinthians 12:7-10), God reminds Him of His grace. He doesn't remove the thorn. He doesn't tell him to "handle it". He tells Paul that His grace is sufficient.

He reminds Paul that His strength is made perfect in Paul's weakness. God reminds him that in the pain of his condition, He's present. When the load is more than you can bear, don't keep carrying it. Cry out to God for help. His grace is sufficient.

Bills, bills, bills (and where your tithes fit in): Reconciling God and your finances

We're in a time of prosperity preaching, so the finances of the Christian has come front and center, but not always in a positive way. As our churches grow and grow, the finances of the congregants that are less fortunate become magnified.

People wanna know, "If the church is so big, why are the people and the surrounding communities so poor?" More importantly, they ask, "If the *pastor* is doing so well, why are the people struggling?"

We're not here to tear any man or any church down, but we do need to explore how we as Christians can keep the faith, while at times struggling financially.

One of the greatest challenges of our faith is in the fact that we belong to churches that depend on our finances to run. We're asked to give at our local assembly, but let's be honest, people are conflicted.

One of the reasons we're so conflicted is because there are times when we have more bills than we do money. To give your money to the church when you have a past due light bill seems ludicrous to someone that lacks faith.

Should I give to the church and trust God, or should I have the mentality that God has already given me the money to pay the bill and

I should let the church take care of itself? Let's talk about it.

The first thing we should look at from a Christian perspective is who owns what. When we look at Psalms 24:1, it says:

> **"1 *The earth is The Lord's and the fullness thereof; the world and they that dwell therein." (KJV)***

So whatever we have is on loan, and it's a loan that we can never pay back. All that we have belongs to God. We're simply stewards of what we've been given. This not only puts what we're doing with our money into perspective, but it should put into perspective who we're giving our money to.

God owns the gas company. God owns the light company. He owns the cable company, the mortgage company, and any other company you're paying bills to. There is nothing outside of His reach, even if they're overcharging you.

Having established the fact that wherever you take your money it's God-owned, we must now establish what God's priorities are. This is where our money, our bills, and our God begins to collide. We place "our" money on *our* priorities and not God's.

The same God that we prayed to and asked for a job or some sort of legal income, we're shortchanging because we don't trust Him or the people He's placed in charge. We begin doing what makes us feel secure. But we must learn to be secure in God and not our homes, our cars, our cell phones, or whatever else we spend our money on.

***

    Now, before we get too far ahead of ourselves, let's talk about what God is requiring of us. If you're a Christian, you're aware of tithing, whether you're doing it or not, and whether it's being taught in your church or not.

You're aware that God expects you to give some of what you've earned back to the church. That's the expectation. It's what God asks of what He's given to you (let that sink in).

If you're unaware, here's what He's asking: 10%. That's what He's asking of you. Out of the 100% that He's blessed you with, He's asking for you to return 10%. For every dollar

He invests in you, He only asks a dime as a return on His investment. It seems like God is coming up on the short end of this financial arrangement.

It also must be clarified and emphasized, just in case anyone gets the wrong idea, your tithes are between you and God first. Many get it twisted and make the assumption that they owe the church. You don't owe the church, you owe God. God has simply asked that you take what you owe Him and give it to the church.

Many are twisted in the church because of this misunderstanding, so I feel I must stress this for the sake of clarity. <u>You owe God.</u> Not the pastor, not the deacon board, not the membership. The church is just the payment center. If that doesn't sit well with you, keep reading. We'll cover that.

Now, back to the 10%. Here are the questions that we must ask ourselves in regards to the tithes: If we're only being asked to give back a dime from every dollar, why are we still struggling? In fact, if He's only asking a dime out of every dollar, why won't we give?

We find in Malachi 3:8-9 that God considers it robbery that we don't pay our tithes. He also tells us that there's a curse associated with not doing so. Again, I'm speaking to Christians right now because that's who The Bible is for. There is a curse connected to not paying tithes.

So when we're trying to figure out why our money doesn't cover our bills as we refuse to tithe, its right there in the Word of God. Consider what I said before: It <u>all</u> belongs to God, you're a steward over what He's loaned you, and He's asked for you to return 10% each time He blesses you. To not do so *is* robbery, is it not?

Concerning the finances of those of the Christian faith, we often struggle because of how we treat God. Many people don't want to tithe because they feel they can't afford to. When I look at those Verses in Malachi, it seems that you can't afford *not* to tithe.

How many times have you kept your tithes so that you can pay all of your bills, and once you'd paid them all, some other expense that can't be put off somehow appears? Happens all the time, and we as Christians ask God why.

However, a better question of why would be: Why would you purposely get on the wrong side of God?

Then there are others that don't tithe because they don't like or trust their place of worship. However, you can't keep what belongs to God because you're mad at the church you attend. If you can't trust your local church to do right with the money you give, it's time to switch churches. The answer can never be to keep what's God's.

If you look at Malachi 3:10, you will see God's response to you paying your tithes. God actually challenges our faith and tells us how He will respond. He says that He will bless us so abundantly that we won't even be able hold it all. So as we see in the text, there's a blessing in tithing. People are struggling in their lives because they're struggling to bring their tithes into the storehouse.

As we go further into Verse 11, you'll see that once you have committed yourself to God financially, He not only blesses you, but He promises to protect what He's already blessed you with.

Have you ever had a bill that you couldn't pay, but your services stayed on until your next pay day, even though you had that shut off notice? Have you ever been low on food with no money, but somehow the food you thought would run out just stretched? There is a blessing in tithing, but there's also protection.

***

Know that God expects more than just our money in the way of tithing. He wants our time and our talents as well. But for the purposes of this section, we stress that financial struggles for a Christian is ungodly. Our struggles don't come because God is unfair, but rather because we're not obedient.

Everyone wasn't destined to be rich, but God has determined that all of our needs should be met (Philippians 4:19). Know that you're financially blessed when your needs are being met, not just when you have money falling out of your pockets.

If that's your situation, you're blessed to actually be a blessing to someone else. But in the cases of those whose money isn't always where they want it to be, God will use those moments to teach us "holy budgeting", if you will.

The Apostle Paul said in Philippians 4:11-13:

"11 Not that I was ever in need, for I have learned how to be content with whatever I have.

12 I know how to live on almost nothing or with everything. I have learned the secret of living in every situation, whether it is with a full stomach or empty, with plenty or little.

13 For I can do everything through Christ, who gives me strength." (New Living Translation)

When we learn to depend on Jesus as Paul did, we will know how to be full in all situations. Giving God what's due to Him isn't sacrifice, it's appreciation for what He's done for you.

And even when it seems that you need 100% of your money to survive, you'll find that through Christ, you can do more with 90% and God's blessings over it than you can do with 100% without God's blessings.

It gets tough when you've got hungry kids and a limited income, and you don't know how you're gonna connect the dots. But I assure you that the answer isn't in keeping what belongs to God.

I know that the mortgage is 3 months past due and they're threatening eviction, but did I mention that God owns it all, including the mortgage company? Not only must we give God what's His no matter what, but we must learn to pray without ceasing!

As a testimony, I once called on a past due light bill and was told by a representative that I have to pay $300 or else. I had nowhere near $300 and didn't even know how the bill got so high since I hadn't received any notice of that amount. I thought I was making arrangements on a $150 bill.

The representative was not budging, claiming she was sure of the amount. I got off the phone in disgust. Then, The Lord spoke to me and said: "Did you ask Me about your bill?" At that moment, I realized that I didn't pray before I called.

After I prayed to my Representative, I called back and got someone different. Her response was, "Hold on sir, let me look at your bill". After placing me on hold, she came back and told me to pay $30 and I would be all set.

Just by talking to God first, He put me on the phone with someone that wasn't just doing their job or trusting what was on the screen. I was on the phone with someone that cared.

Even though the bill was wrong, we all know that I would've had a reconnection fee regardless had service been interrupted, and that's just how it goes. Give God His due in prayer and in finance matters! I'm a tither and I pray. There is a blessing in obeying God.

Also, we must stop telling people that they're "putting money in church". When we tell them that, they connect their tithes with the building, with the congregation, and sometimes with the pastor. These are all things that they don't mind saying no to because all of these things have no power over them.

When we tell people that the tithes are their due diligence to God, it takes on a different connotation with them. They may leave a church they don't trust, but they won't try and keep what belongs to God.

However, let's keep this all in perspective. Many of us struggle because we're foolish with the 90%. There's a certain amount of wisdom that God expects us to have over what we're left with after tithing.

Many of us live above our means and expect God to pick up the slack. We're in positions where we don't have enough money because we're trying to impress people that probably don't really care about us.

It's this kind of mismanagement that will cause us to hold back our tithes so that we can keep up a façade. It's this kind of thing that will have people thinking that God is slack with His people, even though they tithe. Know that God isn't interested in helping you keep up appearances just because you tithe. You have the 90%. You must be wise with it.

In our flesh, we've created some financial catastrophes with God-given blessings by trying to do more than God has prospered us to do. There's stepping out on faith and then there's stepping out on foolishness. If God provides you with enough to buy good clothes, but not designer clothes, be wise. If He provides you with enough for a nice house in the city, don't try and overspend in the suburbs. Living within what God has blessed you with is enough.

Saved people with nicer things are no more saved than you are. There is no separate Heaven for the affluent. The same blood covers us all. We must represent God's blessings on all levels of society. We must show one another that God cares for and provides for all of His people.

***

One of the biggest misunderstandings in the church is in what's done with the money. People often fail to understand or even accept the fact that a church has expenses, just as their homes do.

There's lights, gas, repairs, telephone, and general upkeep for that church that isn't given for free. When you throw in the fact that the church has the responsibility to pay the pastor's salary (believe it or not, pastoring is real work) and do community work, if the people don't give, how will any of this get done?

A place where you can be spiritually fed, come to worship God, fellowship with other believers, get married, and have funeral services for loved ones shouldn't be taken for granted. We are responsible for the upkeep of God's house.

I'm reminded of the First Chapter of Haggai, when the Children of Israel had neglected the rebuilding of God's house in favor of their own wants. The temple of God lay incomplete, while their houses had become luxurious.

God warned them to consider their ways, but He also pointed out that even as they neglected His house, all that they held back wasn't enough because it kept getting away from them.

All of their clothes weren't keeping them warm, and even as they sowed much in crops, they were reaping very little. The point is you can't neglect God's house and get ahead. Even if you appear to be blessed on the outside, it could very well be falling apart on the inside, and if no one else knows, you know and God knows.

The financial struggles or successes that a Christian has are directly tied in to how they treat God and how they treat their fellow man.

Contrary to popular belief, when James 2:14-18 discusses faith without works, that has nothing to do with us getting a 9 to 5, unless the purpose of that 9 to 5 is to be a blessing to someone other than your immediate family.

When you read and understand that text fully, James is talking about the work that our faith produces, which includes helping those in need when we can, rather than offering token prayers.

Again, the overflow is so that our blessings can flow over to the less fortunate. God didn't intend for anyone to struggle financially. He intended for us to be a blessing, not just so that we can be blessed, but because we're already blessed.

Lastly, how you give to God matters just as much as what you give. Scripture tells us that God loves a cheerful giver (2 Corinthians 9:6-8). That means that your heart and your attitude must be right when you give to God.

This doesn't mean that you giving grudgingly won't bless the church, but if you do give that way, you could be missing out on your own blessing. Giving with an attitude or giving with anything other than the purest intentions in your heart is not pleasing to God.

He also states in that text that if you give a little, you reap a little, but if you give plentifully, you will reap plentifully. Your fellow congregant may not know if you're giving a full 10% or more, or if you're giving cheerfully, but God does.

Knowing and understanding scripture

When we begin to only memorize Scripture as opposed to study, application begins to suffer. When you have Psalms 23 memorized without knowing that it's a Psalm of provision and protection, you'll recite it like an Easter speech, but you won't know the proper application in times of crisis, in times when you need God's leadership, or even when you're under attack from human adversaries.

When we reduce Scripture to what I call a "Christian catchphrase", we lose sight of the power that exists in God's Word. When our faith is wavering, we don't know why we should look to Jesus, who is the author and finisher of our faith (Hebrews 12:2). It just sounds good, but we need to know why it IS good. He ran the race before us, and He endured the cross. He knows exactly what we go through down here.

When we reduce Scripture to slogans, we don't fully understand that joy coming in the morning (Psalms 30:5) could take months, and maybe even years. We've got to be willing to dig into God's Word in order to receive its full power.

When we're struggling in this walk of life, it is God's Word that is a comfort to us. However, we can't properly apply what we don't understand. All we'll do is misapply, and when what we're leaning on doesn't comfort us, we either lose hope, or worse yet, blame God.

We're too busy saying "amen" to what sounds good and tickles our ears. A pulpit, podium, and a microphone doesn't guarantee sound doctrine. Giving Scripture in the wrong context causes congregants to do the same, and they do so based on the authority in which they heard it, but not according to the authority of the Scripture.

This is the problem with memorization vs. study. As a society of believers, we're often trying to find quicker and easier ways to do everything. We've stopped attending services on Sunday because we can watch church at home. We've stop going to Bible class because we believe that we can study just as well at home.

We've eliminated Sunday school in many churches because people don't want to be in church "all day" (roughly 4 hours, which is actually shorter than a work or school day). People want an all-powerful word from an all-powerful God, but condensed.

There are some things that you just can't get the Cliffs Notes version of and still be fulfilled. We've got to stop trying to short cut The Bible. There is no substitute for the study of The Word, and no matter what we may memorize, if we don't understand it, any proper application that occurs is just a coincidence.

***

As we go through and try to live this Christian life, we must also understand the role that The Word plays in keeping us on the straight and narrow. Too many of us are living any kind of way because we're not heeding to The Word. We're causing confusion in the church, living below our calling, embracing sin as a lifestyle and not a condition, and all the while we're confused about why we're not as blessed as we think we should be.

Understand that trouble doesn't only come to us when we fail to tithe. It also comes to us when we not only yield to sin, but embrace it, while at the same time, trying to justify it. Not only will the enemy attack the finances of disobedient Christians, but he'll also attack your health, your family, and your relationships if you give him occasion through disobeying God's Word.

So many of us are living lives that are in shambles because we don't honor God in our living. His statutes are in the pages of The Bible, but we'd rather try and live as the world does.

We spout things like "Only God can judge me", as though that excuses us from exercising better judgment on our own. We're far from the call of Christianity and we have more struggles than successes, but we refuse to acknowledge the fact that God is speaking to us *through* our failures. We fail to acknowledge that godly living is outlined in His Word and we fail to recognize that application is how we please God in our living.

We're measuring out our sin in the same way that the world measures out the severity of crimes committed. This is why some things that we do aren't as big of a deal to us as others. Phrases like "It's not like I killed somebody" become applicable when we're trying to downplay disappointing God in our living.

We start to compromise with an uncompromising God. But it is we who have "big sins" and "little sins", not God. We must understand that God has no measuring cup for sin. It's all the same to Him, with the exception of blasphemy against the Holy Spirit (Matthew 12:31-32).

But when we come to realize that God sees all sin the same, that isn't a license for us to recklessly devalue the "larger" sins we commit. That's the time to upgrade the "smaller" sins we commit. They all have the same impact on our lives.

The Bible tells us to hide Scripture in our hearts so that we might not sin against God (Psalms 119:11), so memorization is profitable. But we still need to get back to study so that we know what Scripture goes where.

Furthermore, memorization without understanding can cause us to throw Scripture at people and their situations incorrectly. Because we know it and we've memorized, we tend to believe our own version of The Bible. However, if we don't see ourselves and our shortcomings in The Bible, we're reading it wrong.

I've often said in my teaching that The Bible is not a magnifying glass, it's a mirror. Meaning we'll use a magnifying glass to blow up the sins of others, but not a mirror to see our own sins (Matthew 7:3-5). Trust me when I tell you, we've all got enough to keep us busy without taking on the load of someone else's shortcomings.

In the end, whether we're talking about faith, handling a crisis, or handling our finances, all of the answers are in the Word of God. But we must have a proper understanding of The Bible. Scripture wasn't given for inspirational purposes only. Context matters when you're reading The Bible, just as it does when you're reading anything else.

The reason we have so many misapplied and misunderstood Scriptures is because people refuse to study the time, conditions, circumstances, and the people surrounding the Scripture. If you don't know who's being spoken to and why the words are being said, you will take what you're reading and misapply it to your life and to other situations.

This is not just a problem for the pews of the church, however. Many a pastor, preacher, deacon, and evangelist will not only misapply Scripture, but purposely twist them to further their point of view.

That's why 2 Timothy 2:15 is so critical for the Christian. We must know God's Word for ourselves and not lean solely on the understanding of others. There's no easier way to get lost than not knowing the way yourself.

<u>Chapter 6</u>

The conclusion of the matter

As we've discussed throughout this journey, there are levels to faith. You're not just born into it. You have to be born *again* into it. The struggle of many new converts is in the fact that they must grow in their faith.

When they see those that have been saved for a while, those that have seen God move in their lives in ways they can't even fully understand, they want that level of faith instantly. However, they must understand that it's not an overnight process.

Our faith begins with that saving faith, which is what we confess and what we believe. Romans 10:9 tells us that we must confess with our mouths and believe in hearts that Jesus Christ is the Son of God, that He died, and was resurrected.

If you haven't crossed this threshold, you will be challenged. If you doubt the basis of your salvation, how can you believe anything else that comes with it?

Our faith has to come from what we believe and not church attendance, which is what many of us are doing these days. Faith is not an emotional response to the organ, the singing, or the preacher's "whoop".

It is a belief in the existence, the preeminence, and the power of the true and living God, His Son Jesus Christ as our Savior, and The Holy Spirit as our guide. Our faith must be tied to a God that can handle our lives, our deaths, our finances, our marriages, and us as individuals. It all begins with who you're placing at the head of your life.

As we close out this project, we want to go over some things that will hinder your faith, and some things that will help to identify your faith. I'm an advocate of more teaching than preaching, and if we could just help people to identify where they should place their faith, I believe that we'll create a generation of Christians that are better at exercising their faith.

The failure of faith

If we can be successful in faith, then it stands to reason that there are some things that will cause us to fail in our faith. Let's take a look at 5 areas that are a threat to our complete faith in God:

Vain faith (1 Corinthians 15:12-19) – If Christ was just a man and not in fact the Son of the living God, then all that we're doing is in vain. If we don't really believe in the resurrection, we'll question God at every turn. His existence, His control, His dominion, and His sovereignty will all be in doubt to us. Herein is the reason that many churches struggle, just as the church at Corinth did. They haven't truly committed to the truth of Christ.

Dead faith (James 2:14-24) – Here again, we see in the book of James that our faith is no good if it's dormant. There must be works that accompany that faith. In Verse 19, James states that it's not enough to just believe in God because even the devils believe. However, believing in God doesn't necessarily mean a belief in Christ. Christianity produces the work of Christians. There must be some production that your faith inspires.

Unbelief (Mark 16:11-14) – Even after we're saved, our flesh will at times get the best of us. We often won't believe what we haven't seen with our own eyes, all the while forgetting that some things that we see aren't necessarily true. Think of how often we've seen a kind act, only to find out there was a sinister and ulterior motive behind it. So there are times when we will struggle to believe in the resurrection, simply because such a thing is beyond human understanding.

Little faith (Mark 9:23-24) – This ties in with our unbelief. Sometimes we have a little faith, but we're still unsure. Sometimes we take our issues to God in prayer because we believe He's God, but somewhere in us, we're still wondering if He can do it. This is where we must trust God in the "yes" and in the "no". Little faith and unbelief are the symptoms of wondering if He will, as opposed to knowing that He can, even if He doesn't.

Weak/new faith (Romans 14:1-4) – Something that hinders our churches concerning new converts is our disposition towards them. People come to us after living their whole lives a certain way, and we expect them to transform instantly. We weigh them down with our traditions before we build them up in God and His Word.

At the same time, we may have some among us that are saved, but they still struggle with some things. Let us encourage them in the faith, and look to strengthen where they're weak, as opposed to trying to tear them down with our "superiority".

Answering the questions of your faith

"He staggered not at the promise of God through unbelief; but was strong in faith, giving glory to God." – Romans 4:20 (KJV)

This is what the Apostle Paul wrote of Abraham, but it wasn't always that way with him. He doubted that God could cover him (Genesis 12:10-20) just as you and I did before we grew in our faith. And that is the key. We must grow in our faith!

Through our trials and our experiences with God, we get stronger and stronger. Here are a few questions to answer that can help you to overcome the challenges you may face in your faith:

What is the object of your faith? – This seems to be an easy question to answer, but many Christians are unsure: Do you really KNOW who God is? As stated in my book *An Understanding with God*, many know *of* God, but they don't know God. If we don't get to know God, all of His attributes, and most importantly, all of His capabilities, faith becomes a great challenge.

We must learn to trust Him beyond our capabilities. Which means He can do far above and beyond what we can. He must be at the center of our faith!

So many people still believe that some things are impossible because they can't see how it can be done. Even as Luke 1:37 tells us that nothing is impossible with God, when things don't go our way, we doubt Him. Without identifying God as who He really is, faith in Him becomes just about impossible

Where have you placed your hope? – The old hymn "Hold To God's Unchanging Hand" tells us to build our hopes on things eternal. We must ask ourselves: Do we really BELIEVE in God? Our faith coincides with our hope, and we're often disappointed because we've placed our hopes in temporary things. But temporary things yield temporary results.

We've placed our hopes in the things and people of this world instead of relying on an eternal and all powerful God, who is out of this world.

Hope in God doesn't mean that every prayer will be answered with a "yes" or that we'll never have a day of trouble. Hope in God is understanding that He has it all under control. Hope in God is knowing that He's there, even in the midst of trials. Hope in God is having that assurance that He will never forsake us.

What is the purpose of your faith? – Is the faith you're displaying solidifying your Christianity? Are you growing stronger in The Lord? We can't just exhibit faith in good times, when all is going well. Faith is most useful when God is doing some things that we just don't understand. Faith is most useful when it seems as if things are falling apart.

When prayers seemed to be unanswered, faith should assure you that God is still there, He heard your request, and He does have an answer that will come when it's time.

For all of the things that we may go through in our lives, it is that faith in God that will keep us going. A study of James 1:2-6 tells us that while life will take us through, faith will enable us to get through.

What does your faith produce? – Once you've developed your faith, your faith should develop your works. Not the work you do for man by punching a clock, but the work you're willing to do for God around the clock. We are what we produce (Matthew 7:17-20). We see in Galatians 5:22-25, where the fruit (not "fruits") of the spirit is outlined, that a Christian will produce godly fruit:

- Love
- Joy
- Peace
- Longsuffering

- Kindness
- Goodness
- Faithfulness
- Gentleness
- Self-control

All of these things are a part of one singular fruit. Your faith in God and you allowing Him to work through you will enable you to produce this fruit.

You can't try and deceive God by saying you can do some, but not all. Again, it's a singular fruit. Faith that God can develop this in you will help you to produce what man tells you is impossible.

All that we do as Christians should be for God's glory, and not our own. What faith in our God should produce is that agape love (unselfish, Christian brotherly love) for all of mankind.

When we're immersed in our faith, the reasons we have to not love and care for one another should dissipate in favor of what we should be doing to show that we are Disciples of Christ.

While we aren't saved by any works that we do, Christian faith should produce Christ-like love and Christ-like works. When you love others as God loves you, which is beyond your faults, mistakes, and shortcomings, you can produce that good fruit.

A Final Word

If we've learned anything about faith during this journey, we've learned that we must be willing to endure. When the tests and trials of life get to be too much, we have to become more dependent on God.

The confusion of faith often comes in those times when we feel lonely, as if no one knows, understands, or even cares about what we're going through. But God knows. This is the reason I stress Bible study so much. The truth in how we can make it through is right there in His Word. Not a quick "sound bite" scripture, but the true Word of God.

Isaiah 40:29, 31 says this:

"29 He giveth power to the faint; and to them that have no might He increaseth strength."

"31 But they that wait upon The Lord shall renew their strength; they shall mount up with wings as eagles; they shall run, and not

be weary; and they shall walk, and not faint." (KJV)

What these Verses tell us is that God has a renewal for those of us that endure until the end of a difficult season. Even when we're worn down and worn out by life, God will pick us up.

Waiting on God is not easy, especially when things are difficult, but faith tells us that He will come through. Faith tells us that He will never let us down. His history of always renewing us should be all the proof that we need.

Much of what we've discussed in this book dealt with the difficulties of life, death, finance, and consecration for God's service. However, some of what we've discussed has also pointed to the goodness of God.

Getting to the altar may be difficult, but there's a blessing in marriage. Finances may be tight at times, but giving to God is the first step towards true prosperity in God, which is having your needs met. Being set apart for God's service can be a lonely task, but God will reward those that He's set apart, and those that remain faithful to the call.

As we look to activate our faith, we must understand that doing so doesn't ensure us of smooth sailing on the rough waters of life. We shouldn't look at faith as some sort of safeguard against all of the issues that the faithless have to face.

We shouldn't look to try and avoid a storm that we're meant to go through. Storms come to test the stability of things, and it's in the storms of life that we find out where our strengths are and where our weaknesses are. But it's also in the storms of life that we find out that Jesus will show up in the most amazing way, often walking to us in the midst.

One of my favorite passages of Scripture is one that's often misquoted and misunderstood, Ecclesiastes 9:11. It states:

"11 I returned, and saw under the sun, that the race is not to the swift, nor the battle to the strong, neither yet bread to the wise, nor yet riches to men on understanding, nor yet favour to men of skill; but time and chance happeneth to them all." (KJV)

Now, we've all heard that "the race is not to the swift nor strong", but when we quote it that way, we leave out the battle. Seems like a small thing, but if I train for a race, but not a battle, I'm not ready. However, in the midst of the race, and in the throes of the battle, I have faith that God is in there with me.

Know that in your life, there will be times when you have to run, there will be times when you have to fight, and there will be times when God tells you to stand still.

In the race, you must be willing to endure because it's a marathon, not a sprint. In the battle, there will be times when it's physical, mental, spiritual, and emotional. And then there's the challenge to keep still and hold your peace, when you actually want to go to war or even just run away.

Your faith will be tested, but trust in God, and you'll pass with flying colors. In all of those scenarios, it's good to have placed your faith in the Almighty God and know that He will enable you to conquer whatever you're facing.

You were created with a purpose and a destiny to fulfil. Don't let the enemy get you sidetracked and don't let him cause you to believe that God isn't able to carry you in your weaker moments. You have greatness in you, but it's all tied to your belief and faith in God. It's not enough to state your faith. You must be willing to show it.

Death will challenge you. Finances will challenge you. Relationships will challenge you. Isolation will challenge you. Lord knows, church and church folks will challenge you.

None of these challenges are greater than the God in you. None of these obstacles are greater than the God behind you. No battle is so great that the God that goes before you can't handle it. You're covered on all sides. Be strong in your faith and even stronger in The Lord. When all others have forsaken you, God is still for you!

Be blessed!